LOVE HURTS

LOVE HURTS

BUDDHIST ADVICE FOR THE HEARTBROKEN

Lodro Rinzler

Shambhala
Boulder
2016

Shambhala Publications, Inc.
4720 Walnut Street
Boulder, Colorado 80301
www.shambhala.com

© 2016 by Paul Rinzler

9 8 7 6 5 4 3 2 1

First Edition
Printed in the United States of America

♾This edition is printed on acid-free paper that meets the
American National Standards Institute Z39.48 Standard.
♻This book is printed on 30% postconsumer recycled paper.
For more information please visit www.shambhala.com.
Distributed in the United States by Penguin Random House LLC
and in Canada by Random House of Canada Ltd

Library of Congress Cataloging-in-Publication Data
Names: Rinzler, Lodro, author.
Title: Love hurts: Buddhist advice for the heartbroken / Lodro Rinzler.
Description: First edition. | Boulder: Shambhala, [2016] | Includes
bibliographical references.
Identifiers: LCCN 2016013202 | ISBN 9781611803549 (pbk.: alk. paper)
Subjects: LCSH: Suffering—Religious aspects. | Suffering—Religious
aspects—Buddhism. | Consolation.
Classification: LCC BL65.S85 R56 2016 | DDC 294.3/4442—dc23 LC
record available at https://lccn.loc.gov/2016013202

DEDICATION

When I get quiet, and I mean really quiet, I miss every-one. I miss my dad, my best friends, my dog, and I miss all the women I loved and are no longer a part of my life (not because I want them back, but because they were significant too), and I miss what I used to do when I was young and naive and I already miss who I am now be-cause I know I'll look back fondly ten years from now and chuckle at how I just used the word "naive" about who I am today.

I walk around basically missing everything. It's not paralyzing, though. In fact, if I had to say it's marked by anything, my life is marked by love. My losses, as vast as the may be, are just a part of me. They make me who I am. And at my core I remain whole and complete.

This book is for anyone who has suffered loss—true loss—and could use a friend. I'm here for you. Let's ex-plore this heartbreak together.

CONTENTS

ACKNOWLEDGMENTS

Thank you to Shambhala Publications, who continues to help get my writing out into the world. In particular, Dave O'Neal, who thankfully has agreed to edit all of my books until one of us is met by death.

Thank you to everyone who met with me at ABC Carpet & Home and offered their heartbreak stories. Your stories are the lifeblood of this book. You are brave warriors: Erika, Phil, Lydia, Adrienne, Sandy, Pat, Sarah, Karen, Patia, Patty, Carolyn, Elene, David, Carmen, Sylvia, and all you other wonderful beings. A special thank you to Paula Gilovich and the rest of the staff at ABC Carpet & Home for warmly hosting me in their space for those meetings and to write.

Thank you also to the team at MNDFL for allowing me the time and space to continue to be an author, in particular to Ellie Burrows, who has quickly become like a sister to me.

One more thank you to everyone I love, without whom I wouldn't know anything about heartbreak. Nancy Delcourt, Brett Egglestein, Adreanna Limbach, and other dear ones—thank you for being my web of support all these years. If these books I write ever help another person, it's only because you've kept me alive and thriving long enough to write them.

LOVE HURTS

INTRODUCTION

Well fuck. If you're reading this you're probably heartbroken. I mean, why else would you pick up a book about heartbreak? I'm sorry you're heartbroken. I really, really am.

You know what I wish? I wish so much that I could just write out a top-ten list of what to do so you can fix your broken heart. I can't. That's not how heartbreak works. I think the only way we can get through our heartbreak is to sit in the middle of that terrible, devastating, world-changing experience. This book will tell you how to do that.

I write partly from the Buddhist tradition but also from experience. I know heartbreak. I'm constantly heartbroken, if I'm going to be honest with you (and, by the way, this entire book is me being vulnerable and honest with you). I've known romantic heart-break: some relationships that have ended naturally and others that were cut off way too soon. I know the heartbreak that accompanies the death of loved ones: ranging from my father to one of my best friends to grandparents and uncles and even a friend who died during the writing of this book. I've known the heartbreak of losing beloved pets, and I know that the death of my beloved dog isn't far away right now. I also know the heartbreak that arises daily in the face of massive societal suffering, having worked for the last several years with activists, homeless youth and, well, watched the news more than once. No matter how you suffer from heart-break I promise there's something in here for you, because if I've tasted the widest sampling of anything in my life, it's not whiskey but heartbreak. That said, a good whiskey in small doses can do wonders for a broken heart.

A note about how this book came to be: The vast majority of it was written in the window of ABC Carpet & Home in New York City. Each morning I woke up, went to a private room in this massive store, and opened up my meditation session. Then for the first few hours I would meet with individuals one-on-one and hear their heartbreak stories. I wouldn't offer advice. I'd just be the mirror that helped them see what was going on in their own hearts and minds. Then I'd close my practice session.

In the afternoons I would climb into the storefront window at ABC Carpet & Home and tap on my laptop, channeling the grief and heartbreak that I felt in that moment. This book is a mix of traditional Buddhist wisdom, my own experience working with heartbreak, and the beautiful hearts of everyone who met with me and shared their stories. May it benefit all beings.

HOW TO READ THIS BOOK

This book isn't meant to be read cover to cover like other books. If you're heartbroken you probably couldn't read a book like that anyway. That sort of linear logic of start on page one and keep going doesn't work for the heartbroken.

Instead, you should flip to whatever you are feeling right now. Angry? Go to the section called "If You Are Feeling Angry." Feeling betrayed? Go to "If You Feel Betrayed." Do you think you're falling down an endless well with no end in sight? Maybe check out "If You Feel Like This Pain Is the Worst Thing Ever and No Good Can Come from It." Ideally in this book there is something for each of the many forms that heartbreak may take, offered with the aim that you will go to where you need to go and find a resource to help you out.

I tend to discourage ways you might distract yourself by abusing your body—drinking too much, overeating, and the like. Instead, I emphasize staying with your emotions, getting to know them, and then moving through them. In other words, this book is about you taking care of yourself during this difficult time. I'm merely here to offer ways to manage the myriad emotions that come up during this process and provide a helping hand so you can do that self-care work.

There is so much emotional content that comes along with heartbreak. We'll explore these strong emotions. It's okay to feel these things. I recommend you feel them fully. But a word of caution before we get going: don't think about getting stuck in any of these emotional states. You can go to that strong emotion, set up camp, and spend some time there, but don't get too cozy. At some point that emotion will change, because you will change. You'll move on to working with something new. You might go visit that campsite again and spend some more time with that emotional state, but my advice is not to get too attached to any of what you're feeling right now. You're much more fluid than you think, and so are those emotions.

If you're ready to get into the meat of the book, I recommend looking over the table of contents and going to wherever rings true to you. If you prefer, you could also just flip to a random page.

IF YOU FEEL LIKE YOU DON'T HAVE TIME TO READ THIS BOOK

I get it. You're busy nursing a broken heart and it's hard for your eyes to focus on a page long enough to read a chapter, much less a full book. This book was built with that in mind, though—each chapter is short, and while there is advice in here, there are also stories, practices, and exercises you can engage in so it's not you slogging through yet another book. That said, I'll just spell out what this book will tell you in case you don't have time to go through it all:

You will heal in some form.
Really. Your healing will look different from what you might like it to though; that much I can guarantee.

It will take time.
More time than you'd care to offer.

You will want to be self-destructive during that time.

Maybe you already have been, through drinking too much, having a fling or twelve, getting high, overeating, binge-watching Netflix, or any number of other ways of emotionally curling up in a ball and not looking at your situation. We will go over alternative approaches to dealing with heartbreak, ones that are healthier.

The way to get through this period is to stay with your experience, as much as possible.

Having a broken heart is a bit like walking a tightrope. You know you should just put one foot in front of the other until you get to the other side. Yet those self-destructive activities are tempting. The moment you get distracted by one of them you're going to fall off the rope and it will only increase your pain. The quicker you move forward along that rope, the quicker you will get to the other side.

You can stay with your emotions and not get burned by them.

There are ways to stay with the strong emotions that come up in heartbreak without falling off the proverbial tightrope. You can skip to various parts of the book based on the emotion you're currently struggling with and hopefully that tip/story/meditation/exercise will keep you moving forward on the rope.

Again, you will heal.
You'll get to the other side of the tightrope sooner than later if you can keep progressing, without getting distracted and falling off. Once you get to the other side of the tightrope you'll be stronger. You'll realize you have everything within yourself to be okay.

Assuming you're willing to give this a chance, let's put one foot in front of the other and explore this difficult terrain. Turn the page or skim to what you're currently experiencing. We'll do it together.

WHAT HAPPENED IN THE HEARTBREAK APPOINTMENTS

During my time at ABC Carpet & Home I met with dozens of people, each of whom were brave enough to share their heartbreak story with me. When I entered that series of meetings I assumed I would hear a lot of breakup stories. I was wrong. I heard stories about a million ways that heartbreak can manifest. I learned that the term "heartbreak" is vast and its meaning can include many different types of experiences:

· comparing yourself to others
· reconnecting to a childhood friend, falling in love, and being left by them
· the sudden death of a father while you're in your thirties
· the slow death of a father while you're a teenager

- giving your child up for adoption and not knowing whether he would be okay
- feeling like you may never live up to your potential
- seeing your likeness in yet another victim of police brutality and realizing the same crazy, messed up situation could easily happen to you
- finding out the man you've been married to for ten years is gay
- divorce
- the death of a first love while still in high school
- not seeing your young child enough because of work
- being estranged from your own daughter and grandchildren
- a high-school love affair that ended when the woman went off to college and met someone new
- the death of your great-grandmother a week before your wedding
- not having a boyfriend or girlfriend
- having an abusive parent
- a high-school breakup
- losing your family members (plural) to suicide
- a string of failed relationships
- a partner who is sleepwalking through months of your relationship
- being estranged from your family member due to mental illness
- the loss of a dream home

- the unexpected death of a brother at a young, young age
- the feeling that there may not be someone out there for you
- the death of a beloved cat (I got this one more times than you would think)
- an ex who moves on quickly, while you're still nursing the pain of the breakup
- constant self-doubt
- reconnecting with someone who is the love of your life . . . but it will never work out
- being jerked around by the off-again, on-again lover of many years
- the death of a mother
- being slandered to everyone you know by someone who betrayed you
- losing a sibling to alcoholism
- blatant discrimination
- having no resolution with an old love
- being thirty-nine, wanting a family, and not finding anyone who romantically loves you
- imagining that you would meet God and he would tell you that you squandered the precious gifts he gave you
- being incredibly lonely and not knowing how to be alone
- saying goodbye to loved ones when you move across the country

- a confusing relationship with your addiction sponsor
- relapsing and doing drugs again as a result of aforementioned confusing relationship with your addiction sponsor
- losing your high-school boyfriend due to religious beliefs . . . and over the next two decades never finding anyone else you connect with nearly as much
- the death of your sister . . . at the hands of your mentally ill nephew
- all the people in your life slowly drifting away over time
- suffering from sexual assault
- suffering from PTSD, vertigo, and hearing loss as a result of the tragedy of 9/11
- aging and feeling invisible in everyday society
- unrequited love
- cancer
- thinking that you gave yourself cancer due to negative habits and thinking

These are all things that people told me had caused them heartbreak; I did not make any of them up. That said, I bet there are a number of things that cause heartbreak that I did not hear about. Here are things that those people told me were helpful to them, regardless of the specific circumstances around their heartbreak:

- being with someone who could really listen and see them for who they are, including their pain
- talking honestly about their struggle
- turning their attention toward helping other people
- time (a cliché for a reason)
- spending time with their child
- napping
- therapy
- going to the park with their dog
- meditation (this also came up a lot, including one person saying, "Sitting on a cushion saved my life")
- engaging in activities that they used to do with a loved one who has since passed on
- setting a place at the table for the deceased loved one at major events (and also including the deceased's favorite drink at that setting)
- being seen, really seen, by another person
- tracking down the person they hurt and attempting to reestablish communication
- taking memories and thoughts about a person associated with heartbreak and mentally placing all those thoughts in a smooth stone, then placing that stone somewhere in nature
- yoga
- eating cookies (but not overeating)
- being with their dog

- talking to and stroking their inner child
- reading (including the excellent Buddhist teacher Susan Piver's book *The Wisdom of a Broken Heart*)
- seeing friends
- prayer
- running
- planting flowers in a garden
- dancing
- writing
- eating something healthy, like carrots
- hugging themselves
- breathing into the heartbreak
- listening to the heartbreak

At the end of her story, one woman told me, "I have an ocean of tears, and I'm not a good swimmer." This process of meeting with people about their heartbreak was like being dropped in an ocean of tears and attempting to tread water for a week straight. My heart broke in response to every one of the stories people offered me. I shared in their pain. And, through connecting in that way, I fell in love with each person who came to see me. Thank you to everyone who was brave enough to meet with a stranger and share their heart. I love you. I love you. I love you.

WHAT IS HEARTBREAK?

I suppose if I'm going to write a whole book on heart-break I should at least offer some sort of definition as to what I'm talking about. Heartbreak has been covered in a million different books, seminars, self-help conferences, and more. While there seem to be references to a broken heart as far back as the Bible, some modern resources say the term "heartbreak" originated in the sixteenth century. Dictionary.com defines it as "great sorrow, grief, or anguish," which strikes me as a bit surface level. I'm going to offer my personal definition for the purpose of our time together:

> heartbreak (n.): the vast pain that we suffer in response to our expectations not being met in some way; a facet of reality as a human being

While I was writing this book, people I talked to made a big assumption: that I would just be writing about romantic heartbreak. I do write about it—and if you picked this up because you are going through that, I have your back—but the term "heartbreak" is vaster than just that one scenario. It includes the little ways we let ourselves down or compare ourselves to others. It includes the ways we yearn to forgive ourselves (but don't). It includes someone else letting us down, abandoning us, or dying. It includes the death of animals we cherish. It includes societal heartbreak, ranging from the ways we abuse our earth to the ways we abuse each other on a massive scale. From the personal, to the interpersonal, to the societal, there are many forms of heartbreak. They all seem to revolve around our unrealistic expectations not being met, such as the expectation that "the one" will enter our life and we'll live happily ever after or the expectation that the loved ones currently in our lives will never die.

It would be impossible for me to sit here and address every single heartbreak scenario in one book. But I have found, in my own experience and in my research, that the specific situations that cause us heartbreak result in similar reactions. We shut down. We get angry. We feel devastated. And so on. Those things I *can* cover. So no matter what has caused you to have a broken heart, I hope this book will give you what you need.

WHAT IS LOVE?

In 1993 a dance single titled "What Is Love?" (by Haddaway) swept the nation. It was a simple song, but catchy. The refrain—"Baby, don't hurt me . . . no more"—also identified a crucial connection: love and heartbreak go hand in hand. When you make yourself vulnerable to someone through the act of love, you are making yourself open to all the pleasures of that experience . . . but you are also making yourself open to the pain of being hurt by that person. I don't know of anyone who has fallen in love with someone who has not, in some way, been hurt by that person.

That particular sword cuts both ways: when we fall in love with someone we bring them happiness but there are also times when we will inevitably hurt them too. That doesn't mean we shouldn't love. In fact, we couldn't stop loving others if we tried.

From a Buddhist point of view, love is innate to who we are. When we're hurt we may try to shut down our heart and not be available for love. We want to protect ourselves so we throw up some armor and try to harden ourselves against the world. Yet underneath all that armor, there is always some part of us that yearns to love.

In the heartbreak appointments, even the most guarded gentleman who sat with me blurted out his relationship story and then ended with, "I know I have love to give. It may not be to the woman I talked about, but I know I have love to offer." He's right. Plus, he's not alone. We all have a limitless amount of love to give, if we can get that armor off ourselves.

How do we drop our guard enough to experience this love? My Buddhist teacher, Sakyong Mipham Rinpoche, once said, "True love is the natural energy of our settled mind."[1] The more we are able to settle our mind, in meditation or through other means, the more likely we will be able to touch the love that exists right underneath that set of armor.

In my tradition, Shambhala, we call that armor a cocoon. This cocoon is something we spin to hide out from our world; it's an illusory device that we think will shield us from suffering. It's the myriad ways we spin a web of neurosis and self-protection. We have some really thick thread we create, made out of story lines like "You're worthless" or "You'll never find anyone who gets you" or my favorite, "Everyone else will settle down with someone else and be happy . . . but you." We can armor up a cocoon pretty quickly when we let those story lines spin out, in this radical attempt to protect our tender heart.

Meditation is a tool for snipping the cords on these various threads of uncertainty and unearthing that raw and tender heart underneath. That vulnerable heart is incredibly powerful and strong. It is resilient. It possesses fathomless love. If we can drop our story lines around what a jerk we are, that powerful heart is ready to shine forth and cultivate a life that is full of good people we love and are loved by. Don't take my word for it, though. Try out the practice listed in the section called "What Is Meditation?" and see for yourself whether it unearths your ability to love more deeply.

Four main qualities make up the notion of love in every Buddhist tradition, including mine:

1. Loving-kindness. Translated from the Sanskrit word *mitra,* or friend, the act of loving-kindness is the very act of befriending ourselves. If we cannot love ourselves, we have no hope of loving others. It is like throwing a lawn party and inviting all of your friends. You tell all your friends you want to serve them from your limitless keg of beer. "Great!"

they say excitedly. "Where's the tap?" If you can't tap the limitless keg, no one can drink your beer, no matter how many plastic cups they're holding. The same goes for love. You can hook up with any number of people, or hold the hands of family members, or go on a million dates, but if you haven't unlocked your heart by befriending yourself there is no love to offer to those other beings.

2. Compassion. Having befriended ourselves, we can offer our heart to others. We share in their joy and we share in their suffering. There are many types of suffering we will encounter (more on that in the "If You're Ready to Hear That Life Is Suffering" section). If we can become familiar with the many ways we suffer, then we will be more comfortable accommodating and embracing the suffering of others. We can't just be there for the good times; we need to be there for the bad as well. My personal definition of a loving relationship is one where two people are able to stand shoulder to shoulder together to meet the many discomforts life presents them. That is a compassionate relationship, regardless of whether it is romantic, familial, a friendship, what-have-you.

3. Sympathetic joy. The next quality of love in the Buddhist tradition is sympathetic joy. This means we don't hold ourselves apart from the joy of others, in a

similar way to how we don't hide from other people's suffering. We take on both. Sometimes when we hear someone else's good news we think of how that will affect us instead of simply rejoicing in it. Sympathetic joy is us making our heart wide enough to not just be there when people are having a hard time but in being there for them to celebrate the good times too.

4. Equanimity. My favorite translation of the Sanskrit word for equanimity, *upeksha*, is actually "inclusiveness." It means we remain openhearted not just when we're hanging out with our good friends—we also do so when we see our ex at a bar or that colleague who really screwed us over at work. It means we include in our heart the people we like, the people we really don't like, and the vast number of people we have never even met. The Zen teacher Thich Nhat Hanh has said, "When you love one person, it's an opportunity for you to love everyone, all beings."[2] Making our heart that accommodating— that is equanimity.

Of course, the foundation of loving all beings is starting with taking care of and loving yourself. As the Shambhala teacher Pema Chödrön has said, "Unconditional good heart toward others is not even a possibility unless we attend to our own demons."[3]

First we attend to our demons. Then we befriend our demons. Then we grow to love our demons. When we can truly love our demons, we grow to love all aspects of who we are. At some point in that process, we learn to see and attend to the demons of others.

If we can contemplate and incorporate these four qualities into our everyday life then we will love in a meaningful and truly impactful way. Our love will not be attached to one person. It will flow freely and be available throughout our day; we will offer it to everyone we encounter. We will still get hurt at times, and our free-flowing love may not always be reciprocated, but that's a hell of a lot better than schlepping through our day closed off to everyone we meet. Heartbreak is a part of the experience of love and love is simply a part of who we are. I recommend we become familiar with both.

WHAT IS MEDITATION?

There are many types of meditation out there. Some techniques are time-tested, having been practiced and passed down for thousands of years. Others were made up by self-proclaimed thought leaders last Tuesday. I tend to recommend the former and discourage the latter. I was raised in a Buddhist household and the type of meditation I was taught when I was a child, and have practiced ever since, is *shamatha*, or calm-abiding meditation. Shamatha has been practiced for centuries, and it is pretty wonderful.

This type of meditation is often referred to as "mindfulness," because it involves bringing our full mind to one thing: the breath. There have been a lot of studies done in recent years about this form of meditation, and science has proven what the Buddhists have known for twenty-six hundred years: practicing mindfulness meditation for even short periods every day increases focus, resilience, and leads to a better memory and reduced stress. With every year of study, science adds more to the long laundry list of meditation's proven results.

While I appreciate science backing up the practicality of meditation, I'd like to share what shamatha has done for me: it has helped me show up fully for every aspect of my life. It has helped me wake up to where I get stuck and shut down my heart. It has helped me be more present with simple activity in my daily schedule. It has helped me get to know, befriend, and ultimately love myself. Having established that foundation of love inwardly, I have been able to be kinder, more compassionate, and loving toward others. When I am with friends or on a date with my spouse, I am there, fully. When I have been in painful situations, going through a breakup or holding my father's hand as he died, I have been there fully. It has allowed me to be present with the wide variety of pleasures and pains that life brings.

Meditation has been an incredible gift to me, particularly when it comes to showing up for my own and others' heartbreak. In all the interviews I've conducted, plus my own extensive lifetime of research on feeling heartbroken, I've discovered that the main way to move through heartbreak is to look directly at it and not flinch. To stay with our discomfort is the best way to move through our discomfort. For me, the best way to learn to stay with all the difficult emotions that come up around heartbreak is meditation.

My advice to you is to try it. Sit for ten minutes a day and be with yourself. Don't feel like you need to change yourself. Just relax with who you are . . . for ten minutes! You have ten minutes each day. And I know you can do this.

THE SETUP

Grab some couch cushions or pillows from your bed and place them in an area where you can sit comfortably, without it feeling like you're in the middle of a mess. Pick a spacious part of your home within which to meditate. If you prefer to sit in a chair instead of on a cushion, that's fine.

Set a timer for ten minutes. It can be any kind of timer, including one on your phone. But if it's on your phone set it on airplane mode so you're not tempted to check your text messages in the middle of your session.

That's it. Simple setup, right?[4]

THE POSTURE

You don't need to do anything fancy with your body to meditate. If you're on the ground or cushions, sit with your legs loosely crossed, with your knees falling a little below your hips. If you're on a chair sit in the center of your seat, without leaning against the back of it. Place your feet firmly on the ground about hips-width apart.

Feel the weight of your body on the earth.

Extend upward through your spine. That means you don't lift up from your shoulders. If it's helpful imagine a string at the top of your head, pulling you straight up. Relax the muscles in your shoulders, back, and neck. Lift your palms up at the elbows and drop them, palms down, on your thighs. This is sometimes referred to as resting energy, when we have our palms down. It also gives you a little bit of extra support for your back.

Your head sits at the top of the spine. Tuck in your chin slightly. Relax your jaw so that your jaw hangs open. That should, in turn, help relax the muscles in your entire face.

Some forms of meditation encourage you to close your eyes. My tradition, that of Shambhala, encourages people to keep their eyes open. We are waking up in meditation. We are learning to be present with what is going on, right now. So I ask you to keep your eyes open, resting your gaze about two to four feet ahead of you on the ground in a loose and unfocused manner.

THE BREATH

Bring your full attention to the breath. You don't need to change how you breathe for the purpose of this meditation. Just allow yourself to breathe naturally. Feel your breath as it cycles in and out of your body. Pay attention to both the out-breath and the in-breath.

Breathe naturally.

THE MIND

At some point you will notice that you are distracted from the breath. If you are heartbroken you may start playing out various ways you have been wronged, or future scenarios where you die alone with cats, or any number of doubt-filled fantasies that are not going on in this particular moment. In this moment you are sitting on the ground, safe, with the time and space to be okay with being alone.

When you notice that you have drifted off into thought, I recommend simply acknowledging that and coming back to the breath. If you would like, you can gently and silently say "Thinking" and then come back to the breath.

Keep coming back to the breath, over and over again. If you drift into thought a lot, that doesn't make you a bad meditator. It just means you are becoming familiar with all of what is going on in your mind that day. The mind generates thoughts, concepts, and emotions; that's what it does. To expect it to do otherwise is silly. Forgive yourself any time you drift off, and then come back to the breath.

At the end of the ten minutes, stretch for a moment and enter your day with mindfulness and an open heart.

THE ROUTINE

I recommend setting up a regular practice utilizing the technique offered above. You don't need to try a different meditation every day, although I realize that's something people like to do. Trying a million meditation techniques is the equivalent of picking up a different musical instrument every day—you get a taste of a lot of things but you don't progress in learning any of them. So try this shamatha meditation every day (or at least five days a week) for one month. I promise, you will see the effects of it in that period of time. At first it may be awkward, but stick with it and you will see the payoff.

Sometimes people tell me meditation doesn't work for them, so I ask about their experience. Over and over again I've heard, "Well, I tried it three times and I didn't feel any more peaceful." In our society, where we are accustomed to getting what we want in a short period of time, I understand that desire for a quick fix. Unfortunately, it doesn't apply to meditation. There's no quick version of meditation that allows you to all of a sudden get to 100 percent peace. The quick-fix mentality is like going to the gym three times and being disappointed that you didn't lose ten pounds. It doesn't mean going to the gym isn't working; it just means it takes a bit more time than you want it to. The same goes for meditation.

I recommend you find a quiet space in your home and make that your meditation corner. For me, it's part of an office. I have a meditation cushion and a small setup with candles, images and statues of beings I admire, and inspirational Buddhist texts. I realize that for most people, investing in a meditation cushion is a big deal (although I do recommend doing so). If you don't want to get a cushion for your practice you can demarcate the space by placing a candle, an incense burner, and a statue or image that will magnetize you to that space.

Build the meditation practice into your daily schedule. Some people like to meditate right when they wake up in the morning, especially if that means their kids aren't up yet. Other people do it right before work or right when they get home from work. Others do it before bed. Whenever works for you, build it into your other rituals. For example, you might wake up, shower, put on the coffee, get dressed, meditate, read the news, then go off to work. It just becomes part of the overall routine. After three weeks don't be surprised if it feels awkward to miss a day of meditation once it's become a part of what you normally do.

Gradually you can move from ten minutes a day to fifteen or twenty. But start with this one technique for ten minutes for one month, and watch how your mind and your relationship to yourself and others shift.

Meditation is one of the most powerful tools I've ever encountered when working with potent emotional landscapes like heartbreak. If you disregard all the other advice in the book I hope you will hear this one thing: please give meditation a chance.

WHY YOUR HEART BREAKS

During my heartbreak appointments I learned a good many ways that one's heart can be shattered. However, whether someone told me a scenario revolving around the death of a loved one, a messy breakup, becoming estranged from someone they cared about, or feeling let down by society overall, there was one thing each story held in common: *the heartbreak was based in feeling that things should be one way, and becoming disappointed to learn that they were another.*

Yes, that is the great discovery: things aren't the way we like them to be and as a result our heart becomes broken. Another way to look at this is that we become really attached to our ideas and fixed expectations of how things should be, and when anything other than our specific notion of how things should work occurs, our elaborate fantasy explodes.

For example:

The unexpected death of a father.
This particular story line often revolves around the idea that one's parents are supposed to be incredible super beings who don't get sick and who will live a long life, walking us down the aisle and giving us parenting tips, dying of a ripe old age at home with us holding one hand and our kids— their grandkids—holding the other. A premature death where you aren't even with him and you find out while waiting in line for your prescription at CVS? That's not the way it's *supposed* to be.

Reconnecting to a childhood friend, falling in love, and being left by them.
This is hard; I call it "rom-com syndrome." We have been inundated with the notion that when you discover (or rediscover) "the one," everything in your life will fall into place and you will live happily ever after. You reconnect to someone you knew growing up, they turn out to be great, and you fall madly for them. They seem to fall madly for you, too. Hilarious antics ensue but it's *supposed* to all work out in the end. You could be planning the wedding in your mind when they realize that they aren't ready for a

major commitment and move out. Your happily-ever-after is no longer going to occur, and may never have existed in your partner's mind in the first place.

The death of a great-grandmother a week before one's wedding.
The pain of this scenario was not that the great-grandmother died (we expect people to eventually die of old age) but that it was a week before this big day. The woman I spoke with had a place reserved for her great-grandmother, had envisioned all the things that her great-grandma would say and do (how her friends would find great-grandma so sassy) and what she would drink at the reception. The great-grandmother was *supposed* to see the woman off on her big day. Those things didn't come to bear, because of the great-grandmother's death.

I could go on, but each heartbreak appointment had a distinct arc:

· Things were normal or (sometimes) really good
· Things were supposed to keep happening and/or only get better
· There was a moment of crisis/challenge/change
· One or more people acted in ways that the other person did not expect
· Heartbreak ensued

Some people, incidentally, ended their story by saying, "And now, after time and talking about it a lot, I'm okay. I am healing from that incredible heartbreak and disappointment." Other issues for people, like long-standing racism in our society, were not expected to just stop tomorrow, but people still held out hope that the incidents that sparked their heartbreak might slow or stop over time.

Your heart breaks because life isn't what you thought it would be. At least, that's been the case with me. For example, I thought my father would meet the woman I would marry and my potential kids. That didn't happen—he died when I was thirty—and that was one of the hardest things about his death for me.

That example showed me how we let our minds spin our story lines with "what if" thinking and fixed expectations at all times. "What if I found someone to marry me right now . . . then my dad would have met her before he dies!" Or "What if this person decides they want to spend their life with me . . . then it will definitely work out." If we're on a good first date our mind leaps to the second date, third date, maybe even to moving in together down the road or meeting this person's family. If we're in a serious relationship we think about marriage or having children together. If we have a good friend and they are young we make assumptions that we will grow old together. If we have a family member and they are in good health we plot the next big holiday we can spend together.

But things change. Relationships and people change and expire, sometimes with no real cause (for more on this, flip to the section titled "Why? Just Why?" for one minute).

We become attached to our story lines, including an attachment to being a hopeless romantic, to the way things were, to the fact that you are in love with someone who is not in love with you, to the way things could have been or still could be. Our minds constantly leap to the past or the future, and rarely do we rest with the way things are right now. Instead we perpetuate any sort of thought that involves the way things could be. Because we spend most of our mental energy in the land of What If we are startled and shocked when reality intervenes and shows us the land of The Way Things Are.

In this way, it's not the heart that breaks, it's the ego. Our respective egos are the conglomeration of set notions about who we are, how we respond to various aspects of our life, what we like, what we don't like, and what we really couldn't care less about. You may have started off pretty fluid when you were a kid, open to a world of possibility, but over time you likely have really solidified things.

For example, you may have had an aversion to brussels sprouts as a kid, but give that set notion a few decades of reification and you now have a life where you are set in the belief that you absolutely hate brussels sprouts. That's your undeniable reality. But someday you may eat a brussels sprout and discover you love it, and that you've wasted decades of not enjoying this one thing because of your fixed idea about it.[5] We do this with most of the things in our lives.

It's not just brussels sprouts. We have set expectations and opinions about every aspect of our world—from the types of movies we like, to the types of people we date, to the type of work we should do. A passing fancy becomes an idea, which becomes a way we do things, which becomes a part of who we are. We solidify our life in so many ways through that very simple cycle. That's called ego, in the Buddhist tradition.

If that sounds yucky to you then I have good news: your set ego has an archenemy called Reality. Reality has a master attack plan with its whole "the way things are" schtick, and it constantly shakes our firmed-up ego. Reality says, "Brussels sprouts are really tasty" or "Actually, this person would be really good for you, despite your set notions of who you believe you should date" or "You thought this person would grow old with you? Too bad! He's dead." We feel discomfort and pain, and our response is to say that our heart is breaking, because our set notion of who we are and what our world is *supposed* to look like has been shattered.

Our heart is not physically altered, to the best of my knowledge. Sometimes when there is a particularly traumatic breakup or a sudden death that emotional pain can feel physical, which is known as broken heart syndrome. But really what we're talking about is that the fixed expectations of what we thought was going to happen have been changed. Our fantasies, our fairy tales, our stories that we tell ourselves that all seem so, so real—those are the things that break. And that is what causes us pain.

If I were you, I'd read this and think, "Well then maybe the best way to avoid my ego shattering is to just not let anyone into my heart." Good luck to you! That's not how our heart works. Our heart yearns to love (more on this in the "What Is Love?" section). The head of the Kagyu lineage of Tibetan Buddhism is right around my age and is somehow a million years wiser than most anyone I know. He once said, "The point I want to make is that love can be true and lasting, under the right conditions. . . . Yet often, instead of giving love room to expand, we box it in with our expectations. Expectations make our love conditional on what the other person does or says. . . . For love to last, it is best not to have too many expectations. It is better just to offer love."[6]

We need to give our love room to grow. If we box it in with our set notions of how things should be, we're dooming ourselves to a death by a thousand heartbreaks. If we can relax into the way things are, as opposed to how we wish things would be, then we can engage our life wholeheartedly.

One of the women who came to the heartbreak appointments, Sarah, shared with me a beautiful way that she thought of her pain. "It's like moving," she said. "One thing has to end, so you go through this whole process that's strenuous and sad, and you get sweaty and emotional, and go through all of the things you just assumed you would continue to keep with you, and some you keep and some go in the trash. Then you walk out, with those things you need to keep, and say good-bye. Then, you get to move into this new space, where you can do so much with what you brought with you."

Heartbreak isn't just pain and suffering. There's also an opportunity to take what you learned with you, and apply it so you grow in all sorts of ways. You may end up learning that you are constantly changing, and your ego isn't as tight as you think it is, and that you can actually relax some of that "what if" thinking and become comfortable with the way things are. Those sorts of lessons strike me as incredibly valuable.

IF YOU WANT TO HEAR MY HEARTBREAK STORY

When I told my mother I was writing this book she said, "So this is what we get? Why? Because Blaire dumped you?" I wrote the comment off, as I probably do too much with her, because I knew that wasn't true. On an outer level, I wrote this book because I work with a lot of people who are suffering from heartbreak and I wanted to talk to them directly, knowing that I couldn't sit down and have tea with everyone. The inner level is because I know heartbreak. Yes, we get this because Blaire dumped me but also because of Jackie and Rachel and Amy and Jen and Daphne and many, many other women. We get this because, for a man in his thirties I have known too many goddamn people who have died, many around my age. We get this because every day I read the news and my heart breaks anew, seeing how many people are perpetuating horror and terror on others due to discrimination. On a secret level I wrote this because I need to understand how heartbreak works and writing is how I process information. That's why I birthed this book.

I have many heartbreak stories. There are those surrounding the fourteen years my father was ill, culminating in my holding his hand while he died. There are love stories revolving around major romantic relationships that ended poorly (sometimes at my behest). There are people I have lost contact with, whom I wish I knew how to find. And then there was May to July of 2012.

I have written in the past about my broken engagement, so I will keep it short and sweet.

I loved a woman.

We spent many happy years together.

I got down on one knee and she said yes.

She moved to Chicago.

I stayed in New York City.

I visited.

She realized she didn't want to come back to New York City or to me.

Why? This is always the question we ask ourselves, right? Why did that happen? What could I have done to change it? I don't know. And gradually I became okay with not knowing. Over the years my heart healed and I was able to love again.

A month after the breakup I lost my job.

This wasn't as big a heartbreak for me but I'll be damned: my ego and pride were pretty beaten up.

(Eventually I moved into political organizing, then brought my organizing know-how into a relationship with my meditation work and, in addition to writing books and teaching meditation I am proud to say the Institute for Compassionate Leadership, my nonprofit leadership training organization, was born as a result of that heartbreak.)

A month after the job loss, on July 13, 2012, my twenty-nine-year-old friend Alex experienced chest pain and collapsed from heart failure while he was at his desk in his office. He died shortly thereafter. Here's what I discovered about heart failure: it's the term they use when they have no clue why someone died. Why did Alex die? Well, his heart stopped working. Talk about a case of the Whys. Alex was my closest friend from college, one of the people who showed up for me loyally and faithfully for the good times and bad. He was a true spiritual friend. And I still feel the heartbreak of losing him. Every. Single. Day.

The first weeks after Alex died I couldn't take a shower without sobbing. That's how my day began. Most days I get into the shower now and I still think of that time and of him. There are many sweet things that remind me of him. We stumbled across a love of

Bulleit bourbon. That's my go-to drink now, and every time I raise a glass I raise it to Alex. And here I am, sitting in the window of ABC Carpet & Home, writing a book and mentioning him and sobbing uncontrollably in front of hundreds of passing New Yorkers just because I'm talking about it.

Some heartbreak goes away with time. Some just becomes a part of who we are. It shifts and changes over time, but it's still a part of us. If there's something I learned from those two months, it's that.

IF YOU'RE READY TO HEAR THAT LIFE IS SUFFERING

How totally morbid are you, that you want to hear that life is suffering? I'm kidding. But to be clear, suffering is the nature of things. We Buddhists call this whole cycle of suffering *samsara,* and it is said that we are engaged in it lifetime after lifetime (or, for those of us who are agnostics when it comes to multiple lifetimes, decade after decade).

I remember very clearly a moment in my freshman year of college. The brilliant Buddhist professor Jan Willis was pacing the front of her Buddhism 101 course. *"Dukkha,"* she exclaimed. "Life is suffering. There is suffering. Suffering exists. There are many ways this has been translated." No matter how you want to translate it though, it's the reality of our situation.

The very first thing that the Buddha ever taught was the Four Noble Truths. Truth number one is all about suffering. There are three types of suffering the Buddha discussed.

· the suffering of suffering
· the suffering of change
· all-pervasive suffering

The suffering of suffering is a catch-all for all the issues we encounter as humans. It includes birth, aging, sickness, and death. The birth process is, for all parties concerned, not a cakewalk. For the person being born it's incredibly confusing and disorienting. As we grow older we encounter many pains: the pain of being an awkward teenager, of noticing our body can't do what it used to be able to do, and on it goes until our body gives out on us in various ways. We can experience all sorts of sickness, ranging from the common cold to a whole other C word that I wouldn't wish on my worst enemy. Then we die. Everyone dies. Relationships die. People die, too. Everything ends.

You might be thinking, "That's just the first type of suffering? The Buddha must have been a real bummer to hang out with." Unclear on that one, but he's not wrong, is he? Those are all basic truths of our situation.

The suffering of change is that even the really fun parts of our life are impermanent. It doesn't mean we can't enjoy, say, the beginning of a relationship when everything is shiny and new. It just means we shouldn't do what we often do, which is expect it to always be that way. Relationships change. People change. Everything changes.

All-pervasive suffering is the notion that we are constantly trying to find happiness in the midst of all of these ever-changing conditions, thinking we can be one permanent and stable being and find something permanent and stable to latch on to, when there is always sickness and change and death and all of these brutally hard things going on. Painful instability plus painful instability does not equal stability, despite our best efforts to make it so.

Let's face it: these things all cause heartbreak. When a loved one is sick in the hospital and might die? That's a cause for heartbreak. When a romantic relationship changes and goes south? That's a cause for heartbreak. When a source of great happiness, such as a playful house cat, is taken from us? That's a cause for heartbreak.

Life is heartbreak. It's sad but true. Heartbreak is not something we get over once, like the chicken pox. It comes back, over and over again, throughout the course of our life in a variety of forms. To think we can avoid it is foolish.

The Second Noble Truth, incidentally, is that we suffer because of ignorance and craving. Ignorance in this case is thinking that we will just get better and never have a broken heart again, never suffer from change, impermanence, aging, and the like. Craving is wanting to find some stable happy place or person that will never change, which is totally unrealistic. So that's the reason why we suffer and have heartbreak.

The Third Noble Truth is the "good news" truth: there can be a cessation of suffering. Through exploring all the various aspects of our mind and life we can learn to overcome our ignorance and craving. When it comes to heartbreak it's best to dive in and explore, get to know, and eventually become okay with heartbreak.

The Fourth Noble Truth the Buddha taught is that there is a path to overcome suffering, which includes the Eightfold Path and all the other teachings he offered from that day forward. He was a very skillful guy, that Buddha. I bet he was actually super fun to hang out with. If you want to explore his teachings, I wholeheartedly encourage you to do so; there are many books and Buddhist centers established for that sole purpose.

For the sake of our purposes in this book you will find various practices, tools, and advice to see your way through your current heartbreak, and these are mainly drawn from the Buddhist tradition. The disclaimer is twofold: (1) there's a lot more to Buddhism than what's in this book and (2) the suffering of heartbreak will occur again and again within your lifetime. That's the nature of samsara.

REFLECTING ON IMPERMANENCE

The Zen master Suzuki Roshi was once asked by a student to summarize all of Buddhism in one phrase. He looked up and bluntly said, "Everything changes."[7] Then he moved on to the next question.

THE GOOD

This pain you feel? It's not always going to be like it is right now. I promise you. It will shift and change and likely dull in a big way. While writing this book I met with a woman who spoke about her heartbreak over the death of her father. "The pain will change I know," she said. "Time and talking. Those are the two things that help." We all have heard this though, right? That time heals all wounds? I'm not going to say that to you.

Here is what I have found, particularly having lost major loves of my life, familial, romantic, and otherwise: time changes our wounds. Some may heal entirely. Others we may continue to reflect on daily or weekly and wish they would f-ing heal already but don't. They remain, but we don't become as devastated by them each time we reflect. Eventually we may notice that wound and think, "Oh, that old scar? I got it in my divorce/the death of my dad/ the first time I was cheated on" and almost smile. Almost.

THE BAD

Another thing Suzuki Roshi once said was, "Life is like stepping into a boat that is about to sail out to sea and sink."[8] All aspects of our life, including our relationships, are like that, and for that I am sorry.

Me saying that Buddhists believe that everything is impermanent is a bit like me saying Buddhists believe that water is wet. It is simply the truth. If you disagree, I invite you to go out and find one thing (one thing!) that does not change in any way. The seasons change. Our work changes. Our bodies change. In fact, it's said that all of the cells in our bodies die and are replaced gradually over seven-year cycles so that every seven years we're a whole new being.

Day in, day out, you know you change. You know more than you did a few years ago. You've had different experiences. You have new weird eccentricities you didn't have before. To think that you are this one, unchanging being would be a fallacy.

Here's the messed up thing: most of us take our ever-changing self and partner it to another ever-changing being, entering into an ever-changing romantic relationship, and think that all three of those things are supposed to come together in a way that is permanent and stable. It's like multiplying impermanence times three and thinking we're going to find everlasting happiness. In some sense, it's foolish of us to think that we will go out and meet "the one" and will live happily ever after, based on how much everything morphs over time.

Here are the three main ways relationships end:

· breakups
· divorce (that is, advanced-level breakup)
· death (that is, master-level breakup)

This impermanence isn't just a romantic thing—this can be mapped to friends, family members, cherished pets, and more. As soon as we enter into a relationship with another being we are boarding a ship that will, eventually, sink. Again, I'm sorry.

THE UGLY

Knowing how painful these endings can be, here is what I wish for you: you enter into a large number of beautiful relationships that you cherish for years. I wish that they only end when you all are separately on planes with no cell service and suffer very quick and painless deaths not knowing that your loved ones are also dying at the same time. That way you don't know that they are dying and you are spared that pain, while they too are spared the pain of knowing you died. This is as good as I can hope for you, but given our options it's not too bad. Did I mention I'm sorry?

IF YOU FEEL THAT YOU MIGHT NEVER HEAL

Sylvia sat down with me during my residency at ABC Carpet & Home and told me about the latest breakup in her life, which had brought up a lot in terms of all her previous relationships that had fallen apart. I listened to her intently.

"I know this isn't an advice sort of thing," she said, "But I have to ask . . . will I heal?"

When met with merely my presence she went on to say, "I know. I know I will. I'm strong. I have work to do on my own." I sat there in what I hoped was an encouraging way but kept my mouth shut.

Here's your answer Sylvia:

Yes. You will heal. As another person who came in for a heartbreak appointment told me, "The thing about heartbreak is that you're at the bottom. So there's nowhere to go but up." Another person in a different appointment said, "I realized I can be okay, with or without a romantic prospect. It's up to me to be okay and whole on my own."

If you're going through a big breakup, or the latest in a string of breakups, and identify with Sylvia, please hear me: I believe you will heal. I really do. You have everything in you to do so. While you may not feel it today, you're basically whole already; you just have to discover that.

FOUR QUESTIONS TO ASK YOURSELF

When people met with me for heartbreak appointments, I would sit with them but only ask four questions. Sometimes I would only ask the first one and that would take the full twenty minutes we had together. Often I only got to ask the first two. That was still enough for the person I was sitting with in terms of them moving past the intellectual understanding of heartbreak and getting to the core of what they were experiencing, which thankfully can be cathartic. When given the opportunity to speak and know that they would be fully seen and heard, people didn't need much encouragement; they could go on at length, ultimately moving into their own wisdom around their experience of heartbreak.

I encourage you to go on at length with these same four questions. Start by grabbing a pen and paper, opening up your computer, or (if you prefer) just speaking the answers to these questions aloud.

You can focus on the answer to the first question for longer than the others. Tell your full story, or stories, as much as you would like. It is helpful to declare and thus own our stories. No one else needs to see your answer. In fact, I recommend not showing it to anyone. That way you are writing (or speaking) just for your benefit, without the concern of wondering whether it will sound good to anyone else.

After the first question, put the pen down, close the laptop, or just stop speaking. Sit up straight. Raise your gaze to the horizon. Rest your mind for a moment. Then engage the second question. Repeat this process for the final two questions as well.

1. *What is your experience of heartbreak?*

2. *How are you feeling . . . right now?*

3. *What can you do to take care of yourself in the midst of heartbreak?*

4. *What is one thing you can do today to take care of yourself?*

THE IMPORTANCE OF TAKING CARE OF YOURSELF

There is an old story of a man who was going about his business one day, walking in the woods. All of a sudden he found himself right in the path of a ferocious tiger. He turned and ran, as fast as he could. Just as the tiger was closing in on him he came across a cliff and spotted a vine dangling from the earth. He grabbed it and slung himself over the cliff. Luckily the vine held and he was safe for the moment.

He glanced down to see if he could lower himself onto the ground anywhere. Unfortunately, down below him lay not safety but another tiger, with her eyes fixed upon him. He looked back up to see if the other tiger had left and if he could climb back up. The first tiger was still there. Worse, a small mouse was on the cliff, nibbling away at the vine he was holding on to.

As the immensity of the situation dawned on him, he saw something shiny and red out of the corner of his eye. It was a strawberry, right within his reach. He plucked it with his free hand and tasted it. It was the most delicious thing he had ever eaten.

And that is how the story ends.

Sometimes, when we are plagued by heartbreak, we forget to appreciate the simple things in our life. If you feel like you are trapped between two tigers—that of a serious illness and a serious breakup for example—I invite you to contemplate if there is a strawberry you can reach out for and enjoy.

The strawberry may be a literal strawberry, because those are delicious, but it might also be some other way of taking care of yourself. It may be going to the gym, relaxing in the park, doing yoga, taking a leisurely walk outside with your dog, or reading something silly but fun (I am a fan of comic books myself).

You should find little ways to treat yourself, in the midst of heartbreak. These are things other than the readily available, exciting but potentially draining activities like binge-drinking, crazy drugs, or screwing around. When I asked people how they tend to take care of themselves in the midst of heartbreak, people would almost always open with the thing that they do that they probably shouldn't, like jumping into a new fling or overeating. Then they would continue into all the things that did prove helpful. My advice is to skip the activity that will only make you feel worse about yourself and go straight to self-care.

Experiment with various ways of taking care of yourself. If one feels particularly potent, like going for a run, then try to work that into your daily schedule so you know that at least for one portion of the day you will be taking care of yourself in the midst of this heartbreak.

FOUR WAYS TO TAKE CARE OF YOURSELF

A secret set of teachings were hidden in the monasteries deep in Tibet for centuries. They ultimately accompanied Tibetan Buddhist masters into the West and are today known as the Four Exhilarations. It is said that if you can do all four of these in one day you will feel uplifted and have a renewed sense of energy. Here are the four secret teachings:

· eat well
· sleep well
· meditate
· exercise

Why these Four Exhilarations were hidden away as secret for so long is fascinating to me. These are incredibly simple things that you already might suspect you should do. Yet how often do you do all four in one day?

Eat Well

If you are heartbroken and don't want to eat, please see the section titled "If You Feel Like You Can't Eat." But eating well means more than just eating something. It means not overeating, which is something a lot of us do when attempting to fill the newly emerging and quickly growing hole in our heart. It means not eating trash, like a full box of cookies (I've been guilty of this in the past). It means eating good, nourishing food. When I'm heartbroken I try to eat a lot of protein, soups, and even a salad or two. I'm not really a salad guy, but I know that I need energy to grieve and good food provides that energy.

Sleep Well

If you are heartbroken and are having trouble sleeping, please see the section titled "If You Feel Like You Can't Sleep." Sleeping well means getting more sleep than you think you need. When you are heartbroken, your body is going through a process that is hard and it needs rest. You might believe that you're just lost in neurotic thought—if you could only stop thinking so much about your ex/family member/ job loss then you would be fine. It's not like that. Deep heartbreak is traumatic; it shocks the system and your body needs sleep in order to heal from it.

If you normally sleep for seven hours, you may need nine. If you can't get a good night's rest, it might be worth trying to nap during the day. I recommend keeping a good Buddhist (or other spiritual) book on your nightstand so that if you do wake up in the night you can read a page or two, relax your mind, and enter sleep once more.

MEDITATE

If you haven't noticed, I'm a big fan of meditation. This is because I know meditation can help us. It can help us be with all of the heartbreak we feel and see our way through it. It can help heal our body and mind. It can help us enter our world more open-heartedly. So if you haven't already checked out the "What Is Meditation?" section in this book I recommend going to it now.

EXERCISE

There were times in my deepest heartbreaks when I couldn't bring myself to the meditation cushion. I would sit down and just sob, instead of focusing on the breath. One of the things that helped me get to the point where I could meditate is exercise. Exercise might look different for you than it does for me. I run, go for long walks, or lift weights. For you it might be yoga, cycling, or CrossFit training. I don't think I'll ever do CrossFit. Too intense for me. But good for you! Whatever exercise means to you, please incorporate it into your day.

When you do all four of these in one day you will feel more like yourself and you will be able to engage your mourning process better. We take care of ourselves so we can heal. These are four stellar ways to do just that.

NOT GIVING UP ON ANYBODY

"I'll be damned, Lodro," you may be thinking, having read the title of this section, "if I'm not gonna give up my ex. He is a cheating, lying dirtbag and I am for sure going to give him up . . . the moment I can stop thinking about him every five minutes."

Let me be very clear: there are times when we might need to cut someone out of our life. That person may be:

· a romantic partner who has hurt us
· a family member who is abusive
· a friend who is insultingly self-absorbed
· a coworker who tries to turn every conversation into a way to sabotage us
· a leadership figure who has gravely disappointed or shocked us

I get that you might need to end regular relations with that person. I am drawing a line between cutting off contact with someone and inwardly giving up on them. Heartbreak can mean loving someone and wishing they would go fuck themselves at the same time. It's a confusing emotion because of just that sort of contradiction.

Just because we have been hurt by someone doesn't mean that they no longer deserve happiness in their lives or are beyond anyone's help. I'm a firm believer that everyone possesses basic goodness. The Buddha was a living example of someone who was totally spoiled growing up, then tortured himself in the name of spirituality, only to see that he didn't need to explore external factors in search of peace—he had it within him all along. That is why we call the Buddha the *tathagatha,* or "awakened one." He woke up to his inherent peace and goodness. He's a role model in that we, too, can wake up to our basic goodness.

Let me pause for a second to drive this point home, because it's important: you are basically good. You are basically whole, complete, worthy, kind, and sane. That is who you are, according to the Buddhist perceptive and my own experience of everyone I have met, so I am pretty damn sure it's the same for you, too. Yes, you may act confused at times, but that does not negate your goodness.

When I was traveling on one of my book tours I spent some time in North Carolina. I was hosted by a really wonderful couple. I had never met them before. They showed me where I would be staying and drove me to my event. We made small talk on the way and they were polite but reserved.

That night I was asked a question I get asked quite frequently when I travel and speak on my work: "How can everyone possess the same goodness the Buddha possessed? Surely Hitler wasn't inherently good? Surely Charles Manson isn't basically good? There are people out there who do a lot of evil things!" I answered in the way I often answer: There are many people out there who are very, very confused. That does not mean that underneath their various layers of confusion, neurosis, and pain that they aren't basically good. They are. That means that we need to rouse ourselves to hold compassion and try to create the space for them to realize that they can do good because they *are* basically good. We shouldn't give up on anybody.

Sometimes we may go through a breakup and think our ex is crazy and deranged. Even if that is true, they are not basically evil. They still possess basic goodness, but they are not connected to it or know how to act from it. They are connected to their insecurity and pain. How sad is that? It would be wonderful if we could see that and rouse compassion for them, no matter how hard that might be to do.

On the way home from that talk my host was very quiet. Eventually she piped up and told me a story. When she married her husband they both had children from previous marriages. One of their children was a delightful young man who got involved in the wrong crowd. If I recall correctly, drugs were frequently involved and at one point this group of teenagers got high, beat up, and ultimately murdered a young child. This woman, who is a sweet and kind person, could not believe that she had raised a murderer.

Her stepson had been sentenced to jail and for a period of time she could not bring herself to see him. When she did go see him he was very closed off. She persevered and continued to show up for him in an openhearted way. One day he asked her about the family dog, whom he loved. They were able to share in a tender way their love for the dog. Another time not too long afterward he asked about art supplies, and not too long after that he was back to painting, something he had not done in years. Now, she said, he has softened. She can once more see that young man she had raised, and he is deeply remorseful for what he has done.

"I had given up on basic goodness," she said. "I didn't believe he was basically good." But, out of loyalty, she didn't give up on him. She persevered and showed up for him, offering love, over and over again. Eventually he let the armor around his heart fall away a bit in response and was once more able to become more of who he was. Her faith in the fact that we are all basically good then flourished. What can we learn from this woman? My takeaway is that we should not write anyone off. Even if someone hurts us or commits an atrocity they can still turn things around.

In my tradition, that of Shambhala, we have a saying: "Never give up on anybody." I know I have people in my life I can't regularly engage with because they are aggressive, slanderous, and my presence does not do anything to change that. It may take a more enlightened being than I, or perhaps they may need to go through their own heartbreak in order to soften. That doesn't mean I've given up on them. It just means I don't call them every Sunday.

In the Buddhist tradition we refer to beings willing to keep their heart open no matter what as *bodhisattvas*. *Bodhi* is a Sanskrit word that can be translated as "open" or "awake." *Sattva* can be translated from Sanskrit as "being" or "warrior." It's a person who is incredibly brave in maintaining an open heart, no matter what comes up in their life. This experience is something we can aspire to. The Zen master Seung Sahn once said, "Being a bodhisattva means when people come, don't cut them off; when people go, don't cut them off."[9]

The following example is a little less Zen: but one of the people I met with during my heartbreak appointments really hit the nail on the head in regard to this particular topic. She was talking about her ex-boyfriend and how she was maintaining a steady balance between disliking him and not giving up on him entirely when she met my gaze and stated, "I feel respect for him . . . even though he's a piece of shit."

If you are experiencing heartbreak because of another person, don't give up on them; don't cut them off in your heart, even if you have to cut off regular contact with them. I want to encourage you to hold some hope that they may change. The damage done to your relationship may be irreconcilable but that doesn't mean they are fated to die alone and hated by all. They can still connect to the goodness inside of them and change for the better.

Pema Chödrön is a Shambhala Buddhist teacher who has written extensively about the pain of a broken heart and I can't recommend her work more highly. Below I have adapted an exercise she has recommended. It starts by taking a photo of the person you are having a hard time with and displaying it prominently in your home. This may initially cause you discomfort. So much of working through heartbreak is staying with our discomfort, so that's not necessary a bad thing.

Every time you walk by the photo look at the being you are struggling with and simply say, "I wish you the best." If that rings hollow to you, instead say, "I know you are basically good" or "You're not a jerk all the time." Whatever phrase you choose, make it personal but also make it a way of acknowledging that they are not basically evil. Do this several times a day, whenever your gaze falls on the photo. Let your heart soften toward them over time.

IF YOU FEEL ALONE

Sometimes when we suffer from heartbreak we feel alone. We feel like we're the only one who has ever known this particular type of pain.

There is a story that dates back to the time of the Buddha. A woman named Kisa Gotami lived a hard life, growing up quite poor. Eventually she married and gave birth to a son. She was so happy; the boy was the light of her life.

Unfortunately, her son grew suddenly ill and died. Kisa was devastated. She bundled the boy in blankets and cried out, looking for any means to bring him back to life—some medicine, a healer, anything really. A passerby saw her and advised that if anyone could do such a thing it would be the Buddha.

She went to the nearby monastery and broke through the crowd that had assembled to hear the

Buddha teach. She implored him, asking for his medicine. The Buddha took one look at the dead child and made her a promise: he would save the child if she could find a mustard seed in the city within which she lived. There was a catch, though: the mustard seed had to come from a household in which no one had died.

Kisa was overjoyed. She hurried back to the city and knocked on a door, asking for a mustard seed in order to save her son. The woman who answered the door was happy to oblige. Then Kisa asked the important question: "Has anyone in this family recently died?" The woman teared up. She explained that her husband had died six months prior. Kisa offered her condolences and went on to the next house.

She knocked on the door of the neighboring house and a young woman answered. Kisa asked for her mustard seed, then asked about any recent deaths in the family. The young woman brought her siblings together and explained that their mother had died two years ago and how they were still very much in mourning.

On and on it went, with Kisa going door to door in search of the mustard seed from a family that was not on an intimate basis with death and its accompanying heartbreak. Wherever she went she found people who had lost loved ones—brothers, aunts, grandmothers, children. At some point it dawned on Kisa: she was not alone. Everyone else had lost people they cherished, just like her. Kisa prepared a funeral for her son and returned to the monastery. There, she became a disciple of the Buddha and was able to be of comfort to many people for the remainder of her life.

Maybe you lost someone, or maybe you did not, but I want to tell you that you are not alone. There are other people, in this exact moment, who are sharing the same sort of grief you are. The stories may all be different, but there is still grief. I hope you are able to take some comfort in that.

IF YOU FEEL LIKE MAYBE IT'S NOT OVER

It is, in the way you think of it. Maybe your lover left you. Maybe someone you love died. Maybe you are estranged from someone you hold dear. That version of the person you know and the relationship that existed? Over.

That said, you may find yourself in a new relationship to that person. One of my favorite stories in this regard is in the section titled "If You Can Still Offer Love." You will change and be a different (maybe even better) person as a result of this particular ending. They will move on and change, too. Your love may morph over time. That does not mean you have to shut your heart off and stop loving this person. It may just mean you don't get to see them whenever you want to. The love? You can carry that with you.

IF YOU FEEL BETRAYED

You and this person had a pact. Maybe it wasn't written out, or even spoken, but it was there. You would grow old together. Care for each other. Support one another and lift each other up when the other person felt down. And now look what that person did. They betrayed you.

That jerk.

Yes, it's okay to feel betrayed and think that this person is a jerk. I don't know them, but I know this feeling and it's not pretty. I've got your back. I bet they did act like a jerk!

Here's the thing. I've acted like a jerk before, too. I bet you have as well. Even though you may not want to admit it right now, there's a chance that, at some point in your life, you have done something similar to what this person did to you. Maybe you want to try this exercise I find helpful when I am feeling betrayed. It's called "just like me."

You begin by bringing the image of this person to mind. Just sit with it without judgment for thirty seconds. You can either make this a contemplative exercise or grab a journal and write it out instead.

Either mentally or physically, list positive things that this person desires. Then add three magic words at the end: "just like me." For example:

Becca wants to be happy . . . just like me.
Becca wants to feel desired . . . just like me.
Becca longs for security . . . just like me.

Hopefully that will illicit some form of empathy for this person. Now move on to other areas that might be a bit less easy to cop to:

Becca lies at times . . . just like me.
Becca was totally arrogant . . . just like me.
Becca slept with someone she shouldn't have . . .
  just like me.

Maybe you haven't been arrogant for weeks or slept with someone inappropriate in years, but if you have ever done these things, just own that fact for a moment. Sit with it. If you're like me, you've made your fair share of mistakes. In the instances where we lied or cheated or acted rude, we may have betrayed people we care about. And that either ended that relationship or they were merciful and forgave us.

After a few minutes of contemplating various forms of ways that this person is just like you, drop the contemplation, raise your gaze toward the horizon, and rest your mind. Rest with whatever feelings have emerged.

This doesn't negate the fact that this person betrayed you. You have every right to continue to feel however you might feel. But ideally this exercise will help you move toward some form of understanding for this person. As the Zen master Thich Nhat Hanh once said, "Understanding is the other name of love. If you don't understand, you can't love."[10]

IF YOU FEEL REJECTED

The other day David, a meditation student of mine, wrote me a simple question. He said, "If I'm so lovable, then why am I rejected by the majority of women I talk to?" I have heard iterations of this question before, ranging from "Why can't I find anyone good to date?" to "How come no one seems to like me, for me?" There is a certain finality to feeling rejected, as if everyone else is going to be okay but we're screwed.

I'm a big proponent of the idea that if we do the meditation practice, and get to know and befriend ourselves, ultimately we end up loving ourselves. People are more likely to love us if we've laid the foundation of loving ourselves. It's the difference between showing up to an empty dance hall and showing up to a raging party already in progress.

One you're a bit repulsed by; the other you just want to jump into. That's the beauty of befriending ourselves and setting up that foundation of love. One side effect of meditation is that it helps us lift up the rugs of our various layers of self-doubt and loathing to reveal what's underneath: our innate ability to love and be loved. If you try it for ten minutes a day for a few weeks you may discover the same thing.

But maybe you're like David and question this notion of being innately lovable. You might think, "Ugh. Screw meditation and loving myself. Tell me something more interesting." If you were innately lovable, shouldn't you have found the perfect spouse by now? Shouldn't every lady you talk to instantly want to get your digits and/or jump you right then and there? That's not how it works.

I met with dozens of people to hear their heartbreak story and a number of those revolved around being rejected in some way. Either it was feeling rejected by an existent partner, being kicked to the curb by a lover, being estranged from a family member, or not seeing a place for themselves in today's society. I was astounded that, when given silence and encouragement for merely twenty minutes, these same people got to the point where they would say, "I guess I need to spend more time with myself before I repeat this self-destructive pattern and end up feeling rejected again."

Simply taking a bit of space from our habitual way of doing things proves helpful in preventing jumping into the cycle of pursuing that same type of woman, job, what-have-you.

The more we layer a foundation of self-love, the less petty rejections like not getting a woman's phone number will effect us.

You will be okay. Whether it works out with that person who rejected you or not, you will be okay. Most of the people who have rejected me seem like far-off memories right now. I think if you reflect back on similar times you felt rejected years ago you may feel the same way about that person.

It helps to remember that everyone is trying to do the best they can. I don't think anyone wakes up and thinks, "You know how I'm going to make myself feel better about who I am? By rejecting the people I meet/am close to." I think we all want to be kind, but get a little (okay, a lot) self-involved along the way. Often a rejection has much less to do with us and much more to do with what is going on in that person's own head.

Often we want to make a rejection all about us. And not just us in this moment: us in perpetuity. "I will *always* be rejected by women." If you run that through a Buddhist translation device you might get "I don't believe I'm innately lovable." We have to abandon a lot of the stories we tell ourselves about how we will *always* be treated or how we will *never* find love. The more we can renounce that internal story line the more we prepare ourselves for true love.

Also, if you can muster compassion for the people who reject you, I bow to you. How do we muster compassion in the face of rejection? How can we abandon that internal story line about how we will always be alone and never find love? I've asked some incredible meditators about what we can do other than meditation practice and they have offered me a very secret and powerful teaching that I will now impart to you:

More meditation practice.

IF YOU THINK YOU WILL NEVER LOVE AGAIN

Years ago when I was going through a breakup I called up my friend Brett. He's a very wise man. I lamented that I loved this woman and that she had been callous with my heart. "Tell me," I wailed at him, "tell me that I'll love again. I'll find a woman and fall madly for her and spend my life with her."

"You'll love again," he said. "It may be one woman or it may be many over the course of your lifetime. But I know you'll love again."

That was the most generous thing he could have said.

If you don't think you will love again e-mail me at lodrorinzler@gmail.com with the subject line "I Won't Love Again" and include your phone number. That's my personal e-mail address so I'll receive it quickly. I will call you as soon as I get the message and simply tell you what Brett told me: "You will love again. I promise." Sometimes we just need to hear it.

IF YOU FEEL LIKE A FAILURE

I turned thirty on November 22, 2012. If you're curious about what pain I was feeling that day check out the "If You Want to Hear My Heartbreak Story" portion of this book. The short form is, I was reeling. I was newly liberated from the only thing that had been distracting me from my grief: a temporary job as a field organizer for Barack Obama's presidential campaign. He had gone ahead and won reelection, which was nice and all, but that meant that all of us campaign staff had to go back to our normal lives or start new ones. I wasn't sure I was ready for either. I was still mourning the triple loss of my fiancée, my full-time job, and my best friend.

I woke up that morning and walked into the bathroom. I turned on the shower. I couldn't bring myself to get in. I felt like such a failure. Here I was, thirty years old, with no job, little to no savings, a failed engagement, and on top of my personal failures, one of my best friends had just died. I thought about it selfishly for a minute: "Geez Alex. I could've used you today but you had to go and die on me." It's embarrassing to admit I was so self-centered, but in that moment, I leapt into the "I'm a failure" inner monologue black hole and flailed about there. I thought that if I got into that shower then that would mean I accepted starting my day, which would mean I accepted turning thirty, which I simply did not want to do.

So I stood there for several minutes. I wallowed. In that time I did not acknowledge that my first book was out in the world, that people were writing me regularly to say it was helpful, or that I was already under contract to write a second. I didn't think about the close friends who were still alive who I would see later that day. I didn't think about the women who were interested in pursuing a relationship with me. I didn't have the mental space to contemplate anything that one might argue would constitute a lack of failure; I could only think about what I had lost and how everyone else had their act together but me. I thought in particular that the dissolution of my engagement meant that I had failed at love (and everyone knew it). Then I got over myself, let that story line go, got in the f-ing shower, and got ready for my day.

We all feel like a failure at some points in our life. It might be because our romantic relationship ended and all of our friends and family are pitying us in really patronizing ways. It might be because we thought we would have accomplished more in our work by now. It might be because we didn't do something we should have, and that caused a situation to spiral out of control. No matter what the circumstances may be, this feeling can be heartbreaking.

The heartbreak of feeling like a failure is rooted in the ways we perpetuate self-doubt. I have been studying Buddhism my entire life. My experience of applying these teachings to when I feel like a failure can be boiled down to one simple question: how much can you believe in yourself versus how much do you sit around doubting every aspect of who you are? I don't mean "self" in the vein of an eternal, permanent self. I mean the core of who we are: our basic goodness. How much can we actually develop confidence in that? Because if we can't, then we walk around constantly questioning ourselves, comparing ourselves with others, and thinking we're a failure while everyone else has it all figured out.

From an early age we are conditioned to think that we're not good enough. There are movies, magazines, and advertisements surrounding us, subliminally telling us we should look or be different. These various voices combine into one big shout in our ears: "You're not good enough! Look outside of yourself for fulfillment!"

The other day my partner was on the subway when she witnessed a horrifically awkward scene. A young girl, maybe five years old, pulled on the sleeve of her father and pointed at a subway ad showcasing the "perks" of breast augmentation. On the ad there are two photos of a woman. In the first one she is holding lemons up over her bare breasts and she looks very sad. In the second one she is holding up large cantaloupes over the same region and looks very happy. "Daddy," the little girl imploringly asked, "why is that woman sad in that first photo but happy in the other one?" The father, to his credit, handled it well. He asked his daughter why she thought she might be sad and then steered the conversation away from the ad into a more general conversation.

I had seen that ad before and found it tasteless but this story really illustrated to me how we are indoctrinated from a young age to think in certain ways. In this case the young girl was taught that if she grew up to have small breasts she would be unhappy. But if she ended up with larger breasts (or better yet, went to the doctor advertised to get larger breasts) she would be really happy. How yucky is that?

This ad is just one of a million voices adding to that big shout of "You're not good enough! Look outside of yourself for fulfillment!" We are constantly surrounded with smiling visions of people who are better-looking, happier, richer, and more romantically successful than us. Pick up any *People* magazine and you will begin to compare your life to a seemingly perfect one. Yet if you ever sat down with your favorite celebrity featured in this magazine I think they would be the first to tell you that they don't have it all together by any means. They may even say they, too, often feel like a failure in ways you may never have suspected.

One of the ways that I and other people I've talked to have brought heartbreak on ourselves is through comparing ourselves with others. It is through looking around and thinking that everyone else has their act together—and we're the only one who doesn't—that we perpetuate this feeling of being a failure. If we're all walking around thinking we're failures but actually doing cool stuff and spending time with loved ones, I have to wonder . . . are we? No. No we're not.

You're not a failure just because things didn't go the way you imagined. It's time to ignore the shout of society telling us we need to look for things outside of ourselves to complete ourselves. It's time to replace that shout with our own voice saying, "You are basically good and you have everything you need inside of yourself to be successful." Let's stop comparing ourselves to others. Let's set aside the story line about why we're a failure. Let's choose instead to embrace the many ways we are successful. The important thing is that you define what success means to you. I recommend you go straight into the journaling exercise in the following section.

JOURNALING EXERCISE FOR WHEN YOU FEEL LIKE A FAILURE

Do you have anyone who loves you? I bet you do. If you answered no, think hard. Maybe you have a cat or a dog who simply adores you? Once you've come up with the image in your mind of this person or animal, sit with that image for a few moments. You are fortunate. You are wealthy in love. Sometimes we need to be guided to see our wealth, though. If you feel like you have failed in one aspect of your life—work, romance, family, whatever—then I encourage you to sit down and break out your journal.

Write out what you think you have failed at. Go on, it won't hurt you. Sometimes simply writing something out has a liberating effect on us.

Now, on a new piece of paper, write out a header of some other aspect of your life. If you were like me and thinking you've failed at love, then write

FRIENDS or WORK or another area of what you do and who you spend time with. If you're stuck just think about who you've talked to in the last week and that might give you some leads.

Under that header, list out the ways you are wealthy. If the header is FRIENDS, jot down the names of friends you love and maybe even something you love about them. If it's WORK, list some of the things you are proud of in your work. Whatever it may be, put it down. Do it free-form; no particular order is necessary for this exercise.

When you feel a sense of completion, read your list aloud, slowly. Rejoice in your good fortune to have such success in friendship, work, family, or other areas of your choosing.

One final step. A fun one. Read the piece of paper that lists your failure aloud. Feel the weight of those words. Take a deep breath . . . and burn that piece of paper. Let the story line around why you are a failure go in that moment.

Take the paper that lists how you are spiritually wealthy and set it aside somewhere you can see it again in the future. If you want, you can even frame it and place it on your desk or dresser. Rejoice in the many people who have your back and the many ways you experience success.

IF YOU FEEL LIKE THIS PAIN IS THE WORST THING EVER AND NO GOOD CAN COME FROM IT

A long time ago, there was a farmer who had a lovely family and a modest farm, which included one horse.

One day they woke up to find that the horse had run off. Members of the family mourned the loss of the horse and neighbors comforted them, sharing in their sorrow. The farmer simply shrugged. "We shall see," he said, "whether this is a good thing or a bad thing."

A week later, the horse returned! And in good company no less. Accompanying the horse was a wild mare, which was easily tamed. Now all the neighbors clamored around, congratulating the farmer on his good luck. The farmer admitted he was happy about it, but again shrugged. "We shall see whether this is a good thing or a bad thing."

A while after, the farmer's son was racing one of the horses across their fields when he fell off and broke both of his legs. He was patched up by the local doctor but was in a lot of pain. The neighbors again came around, offering condolences for the family's poor fortune. "He's alive," said the farmer. "He will heal. We shall see whether this is a good thing or a bad thing." The neighbors must have wondered about him—how could this possibly be a good thing?

The next week, a battalion of soldiers came through town, recruiting for a war that was already under way. All the men of fighting age were immediately drafted . . . save one. The farmer's son was spared, as he couldn't even walk yet. All the heartbroken families who had sent their sons to war looked to the farmer, noting that he was indeed a fortunate man after all. The farmer said nothing at all.

We do not know what will come out of our pain. I have talked to many people about their heartbreak. Most of them end the story with "but I never would have . . ." The "never would have" could be "never would have met my current husband" or "never would have reconnected with my family member" or, in my case with the loss of my friend Alex, "never would have founded my nonprofit organization or my meditation studio."[11] One person actually said that he experienced heartbreak in a similar way to a bone breaking—it hurt like hell, but it ultimately healed and he was stronger than before as a result.

Does whatever good come from the heartbreak somehow justify it? More often than not, no. But that doesn't mean that absolutely no good will come from your pain. You may just have to wait to see what happens, just like the patient farmer.

IF YOU CAN'T BELIEVE THIS HAS HAPPENED

It has. And you will be okay. I promise you; you will get through this. The view of basic goodness isn't just that you are basically whole and innately good. It's that you have everything you need inside of you to see your way through whatever seemingly insurmountable pain it is that you are feeling right now. Step one? Acknowledging that this situation has come to pass. You can acknowledge it. Say it aloud. Write it down. Do something to at least make a gesture of acceptance that this has occurred.

Step two is not acting out in a way that will perpetuate your pain. As my friend and wonderful Buddhist teacher Sharon Salzberg once told me, "Some things just hurt. And . . . we can make them a whole lot worse." If you hurt, that's one thing. But don't perpetuate your suffering by acting out and making yourself feel worse.

Step three is taking care of yourself, to the best of your ability.

Step four is offering me a modicum of trust here when I tell you that you will be okay.

IF YOU SUSPECT IT'S TIME TO CUT SOMEONE OUT OF YOUR LIFE

You're probably right. It doesn't mean you give up on them (see more on that in the "Not Giving Up on Anybody" section). But sometimes you have to create some space from someone in order to be able to breathe properly. While I was at ABC Carpet & Home I met with a woman, we'll call her Laney, who shared with me one of the more wild heartbreak stories I've heard.

Laney is twenty-eight and met Bill when she was a freshman in college. She had a major crush on him, which only deepened as they became friends. One night at a party she saw Bill kissing her best friend. Bill and this friend began dating thereafter. She was heartbroken.

Our story only begins at that initial moment of heartbreak. Laney went on to date a young man named Stanley. She still carried strong feelings for Bill, but the two were merely friends, part of a tight-knit social group that continued after college. Laney remained with Stanley; although they went in different directions at times, they often returned to one another as lovers. One night in New York City, Laney and her new best friend, Serena, scored some ecstasy and entered into what Laney describes as a "heart wide open" state. They went to a party where Serena and Bill began making out—but triggered by the incident from her freshman year, Laney interjected and hooked up with Bill instead. Serena and Stanley hooked up that night as well.

From that night on, Laney was dating Bill. Stanley seemed to have moved on relatively well, remaining friends with Laney despite the whole ecstasy incident.[12] After the years of buildup, the relationship between Laney and Bill got rocky real quick. They broke up, got back together again, and on it went in a tumultuous will-they, won't-they manner.

Generally in these heartbreak appointments I was able to rest and be fully present with the other person. With this one, however, I remember distinctly, about halfway through the story, thinking, "It's like the TV show *Friends*—a small cast of people rotating in various romantic setups over many years." I was enthralled.

The relationship problems came to a head when Laney and Bill decided to move to Santa Fe together. Laney uprooted her life, moved out there, and a week in was eagerly awaiting Bill's arrival. He'd been dodgy though, avoiding her calls. Finally it came out that he had met someone else and had fallen in love with her. Compared to other trouble they had had in the past, this was a very public breakup; Laney had told everyone that she was moving with Bill to Santa Fe and had set up a home for them there.

The camel's back was broken by this particular straw. Laney told me that she couldn't see Bill for some time, and the thought of running into him and his girlfriend brought her so much anxiety she thought she would have to go to the hospital. She ended up isolating herself from friends and was miserable.

I was not surprised to hear that when his latest girlfriend dumped Bill a week before his thirtieth birthday he and Laney got back together. If this is beginning to sound like a soap opera, I get it. I ended up thinking the same thing. That cycle of the relationship lasted only a little while, then they broke up because, according to Bill, he had gotten too good at hurting her.

Laney may not be able to see the cycle of pain and heartbreak she's a part of, but she does see the value of this person. She can't separate from him entirely and it's causing her a lot of pain. When she left me she was preparing to go out to dinner with Bill that night. They were celebrating ten years of friendship. He has been a major influence in her life and this relationship has showed her a lot about how she loves. She left, saying how the relationship was actually quite a positive thing despite all the pain that it's wrought in her life. It strikes me that this relationship, whether it be friendship or romantic, seems to be eating her up inside and causing her a lot of grief.

If you're reading this story and you think it's in some small way describing you and your paramour, I would recommend taking some time to yourself. If you suspect it's time to cut this person out of your life, do it. Take some time to get to know and befriend yourself independent of this life-changing and emotionally charged relationship. Cut them out, at least as an experiment, and be on your own for a bit.

Meet new people. Kiss someone else, or at least flirt. Expand your horizons beyond the few people you seem to be orbiting around. Even *Friends* benefited from introducing new cast members at the end. And look how happy Phoebe was, marrying outside of the main cast. New is sometimes very good. You may find that by taking some space from this person, you are more able to heal your broken heart.

WHY? JUST WHY?

One day a meditation student approached the Zen master Suzuki Roshi crying, clearly in pain. The student yelled out, "Why is there so much suffering?" Suzuki Roshi replied, "No reason."[13]

IF YOU FEEL LIKE YOU CAN'T EAT

You're heartbroken. You might be thinking, "Who cares if I eat? I'm not even hungry. I'll lose ten pounds by not eating, combined with a healthy dose of crying and shaking from rage and then should I ever run into my ex in the street I'll simply look fantastic."

Here's what I ask of you: eat. Eat something. Anything.

Ice cream works. You don't even have to chew it. Or put it into a bowl. Who needs a bowl? Eat it from the container. Just put a spoon in, lift it into your mouth, drop that sucker of a spoonful in, and it will go down. That's very little effort.

If you share my proclivities when heartbroken you might read this and say, "You know what else doesn't need to be chewed? Alcohol!" This is true.

But I don't recommend drinking if you haven't eaten. You'll only get hungover and feel even worse than you do now.

At least have a sandwich before your alcohol, now that I've put that thought in your head. I like grilled cheese myself.

But seriously, eat. Look at you. You're wasting away! Eat something! I'll wait.

Good. Now, because I'm not sure if I believe you, e-mail me what you ate. Bonus points for pictures to prove it. I'm reachable at lodrorinzler@gmail.com and will write you back.

Now at least you have some sustenance so you have energy to really mourn.

IF YOU FEEL LIKE YOU CAN'T SLEEP

Sometimes it feels impossible to sleep. You know you need to; your body craves it. But you're too angry/stressed/sad to relax to the point where you can lie still. I hope this meditation will help you sleep; it has helped me in the past. I recommend reading about it, getting a feel for what you should do, then setting the book aside and doing it.

Move your electronics away from your bed, perhaps even removing them from your bedroom. Silence your phone. The last thing you need while trying to rest is a series of screens lighting up, potentially with news about whatever is already keeping you up. This is a bit out-of-sight, out-of-mind, but removing the temptation to continue to engage other people about whatever story lines fill your head may prove beneficial. In this way you slow down your mental activity before you even hit the covers. That can be a relaxing way to enter this particular meditation.

Now, lie down in bed. Lie on your back and stretch your body out. Lift and stretch your legs gently. Place your hands either behind your head or rest them on the center of your stomach, palms down. Relax the muscles around your eyes.

Start by taking three deep breaths: in through the nose, out through the mouth. Even in these first few breaths you may notice that your mind begins to think through all the things you have to do the next day. Those are thoughts about the future. Let them go. Return your attention to the natural cycle of your breathing.

Thoughts of your past may also arise. You may be thinking of things you did not get done today or things you wish you could have said. Let those thoughts go. Return your attention to the natural cycle of your breathing.

If there is one specific topic that continues to arise, take sixty seconds to look at that story line. Let it play out for that period of time. But stay focused on that particular story line. Do not let your thoughts stray beyond that specific issue or topic. After that one minute, take those three deep breaths again and then return your attention to the natural cycle of your breathing. Close your eyes and rest.

If you are still feeling far from sleep, you can do a short body scan.

Begin by bringing a sense of awareness to the muscles in your feet and legs. Allow those muscles to relax. Slowly move your attention up through your legs into your torso, allowing the muscles there to relax around your hips and your butt. Continuing up, relax the muscles in your back, your shoulders, and your chest. Bring the same awareness and relaxation to the muscles in your arms, in your hands, and up to the tips of your fingers.

Relax the muscles in your neck. That may mean moving your head back and forth, stretching it a bit. Bring a sense of ease to the muscles around your forehead, uncreasing your forehead, relaxing the muscles around your eyes and your nose and around your jaw. If you relax your jaw and it hangs open that actually helps relax the other muscles in your face. Return to the awareness of the muscles around your eyelids, allowing those to relax and close. And then come back to the breath.

You do not need to contort or move your body in any way. You only need to allow it to relax in its existent state. Breathe. Sleep contentedly.

IF YOU'RE TEMPTED TO GO HOP IN BED WITH SOMEONE

Don't. I mean, it will probably be fun for a little bit but then you wake up and you're all confused about what's going on and you're likely hungover and trying to figure out who that was and whether it was even good sex. It's really not worth it.

Particularly if you're feeling rejected by another human being, you might get the impulse to open yourself up to someone else's affections by getting sexual way too soon. You don't have to do it. Here, let me disgust you a bit and you'll see what I mean.

Years ago I met someone who showed me the pain of this particular temptation. It was during a time when I was suffering through a breakup and I found myself at my local bar at the end of a long night out with friends. I had a few drinks and was considering this sort of distraction, if I'm going to be honest. I was seated next to a woman who was clearly enjoying the attention of a man. When he excused himself to the restroom she sighed, bored, and looked around the room. Something rang a little bit off to me, so after a few minutes of being friendly I asked her about the guy. "He's my ex's friend," she said. "My ex cheated on me so, even though I think this guy is a boring creep, I'm going to give him a night he won't forget. This isn't even the first of my ex's friends. That asshole will feel my revenge."

I was shocked that my simple question revealed such an answer. I mean, that's some dialogue out of a bad movie right there: "That asshole will feel my revenge." The gentleman returned, and I excused myself back to my drink. I went home (alone, thank you for asking) but I couldn't sleep. I was heartbroken, newly single, and hated the idea that this was some perverted option that everyone but me knew existed: just sleep with your ex's friends, then you'll supposedly feel good again. The logic around this particular situation was driving me crazy and didn't seem to add up. Just because she was hurt by this guy she would set out to ruin all of his friendships? That would somehow make her feel healed and loved again? The whole situation was beyond my level of comprehension.

The woman, Kate, had told me she worked nearby and invited me in, so I walked to her place of employment the next day. She was glad to see me, and she clocked out so that we could get a coffee. After getting to know each other a bit more, I asked her a few questions about her situation and this guy.

"Look," Kate said, starting to become annoyed she had befriended such a judgmental Buddhist teacher, "I know what I'm doing is not healthy. I know that me getting in bed with other guys, particularly his friends, isn't going to make me happier. After a few of his friends now I actually feel worse. But I did it and now we both feel bad."

She wanted revenge. I got that. I can't deny the impulse to want someone who has hurt you to feel some semblance of your pain. That said, I don't condone what Kate was doing. The only saving grace from the situation is that I didn't have to be the new friend scolding her; she knew this wasn't a meaningful way to deal with her pain and decided to stop doing it all on her own. I followed up with her and instead of continuing on that self-destructive path, she decided to take some time to herself.

I think sometimes when we feel rejected we have this impulse to get over our ex by getting under someone else. We don't need to do that. In fact, we're missing a crucial alternative: we can just rest with our loneliness and feelings of rejection (more on this in the "If You Feel Rejected" section). I realize that doesn't sound as exciting as jumping someone.

When we are feeling hurt we can do something radical: we can just feel hurt, without having to *do* something (or someone) about it.

Sometimes when we feel hurt by another person, we begin to question whether they even loved us at all. I know that one: where you are in a relationship and that person ghosts on you. Then you begin to question whether all those month or years of happiness were entirely fabricated and only on your end.

Was your love not even real? It was, I promise. The head of the Kagyu lineage of Tibetan Buddhism, His Holiness the Seventeenth Karmapa, offered some advice on this topic. He said, "I have observed a strange idea of love that many people seem to have: they see love as a kind of gift that has to be given back. . . . But love doesn't always have to be reciprocated. We can just love. If love doesn't come back to you, it is still love that you give and that you feel."[14]

Even when your spouse leaves, it doesn't mean the love is no longer there. The love remains. To play off the Karmapa's analogy, if you gave someone a gift and they died, would the gift no longer exist? No, it would still be there sitting in their home, even if that person no longer owns it. The same can be said for our love. Just because the person we love is no longer there actively receiving and echoing back the love, it doesn't mean the love itself dissolves.

When you feel rejected, hurt, and want to act out on that by seeking some form of revenge please remember what the Karmapa said. We can just love. I don't mean this in some hippie way; what I'm saying is that we can just relax and touch whatever lingering feeling of love still exists underneath our layers of pain and hurt. Even though that person may no longer be with us, and that love we have is not being reciprocated, it doesn't mean it didn't exist before or that it doesn't exist now. In this moment, instead of trying to find love outside of yourself, please just see if you can drop right below the surface of your pain and feel the love that still exists.

IF YOU FEEL ASHAMED

There's a funny thing that happens whenever I give meditation instruction. I'll be chatting with someone afterward and ask them about their experience. They will say it was nice, or interesting, or be honest and say it was a bit hard to do. "But I felt bad," they will inevitably say, "because I was fidgeting so much." The thing is, as I'll often reply, no one noticed their scratching that itch but them. Everyone else was too self-involved in trying to be a good meditator and felt equally embarrassed and ashamed when they scratched an itch or their stomach rumbled.

If my small meditation studio is any indication of society overall, then one conclusion I can draw is that we tend to walk around thinking everyone knows our current shame and can read it plain as day on our faces. We believe everyone is looking straight at us and seeing our inner turmoil; the reality, however, is that they are completely wrapped up in their own internal drama and aren't paying us any heed at all.

If you are feeling shame, for leaning too hard on loved ones or for having a broken heart or for bursting into tears at the end of yoga, don't feel like you are alone. Other people are going through similar things. I actually think crying on the subway is an old New York City tradition, yet every time I see someone do it they clearly think they invented that gig and are blatantly ashamed to be doing it. I try to make a point of reaching out to those people, letting them know I've been there, in the hopes that they might relinquish that sense of shame around crying in public.

I remember an instance years ago, where I was lying in bed with a girlfriend and a simple conversation around summer plans quickly escalated into a breakup. Because we were both bewildered about how things had progressed to that point so quickly, we decided to take a walk and talk things out. We wandered aimlessly, eventually ending up sitting on a park bench. One or both of us began to cry; that part is all a bit of a blur to me now.

The one thing I do remember is that a middle-aged couple wandered over to us, clearly lost, and asked for directions. I thought to myself, "Can't they see we're going through a breakup? How incredibly horrible of them to approach us, instead of anyone else in this park." Yet they didn't realize what was going on with us; they just knew they were late and were wrapped up in being lost. We were merely extras in the movie of their life.

What I learned in that moment is that everyone is wrapped up in their own stuff, so 90 percent of the time they won't even notice whatever you might feel ashamed about. The 10 percent of semiobservant people who see your pain will likely empathize with you. Having seen that you are having a hard time and knowing that they have experienced similar things in the past, their hearts may very well go out to you. They might hold a door open for you or offer you tissues. They are not pitying you, necessarily; they are extending their whole being to you.

To reiterate what I've said elsewhere in this book: you feel what you feel. There is no shame in feeling those things. If you can, even for a second, look that shame in the eyes and let it go, you will be able to move through your vast emotional landscape less encumbered. You do not need to feel ashamed for leaning on people, for public displays of emotion, or for being who you are. You can drop the shame and return to this present moment, feeling whatever is coming up in your body. Like many things in this book, this is simple advice but not always easy to follow. I believe you can do it. The first step is realizing that you are not alone: everyone else is suffering right alongside you.

IF YOU FEEL LIKE YOU MIGHT NEED A GOOD KICK IN THE PANTS

Maybe you're being a bit indulgent, lying in bed and moaning about your lost love. Maybe you have binge-watched more seasons of television than is good for you. Maybe you're really, really hungover but keep going back to the bottle so you can drink yourself to forgetfulness. If so, here's a kick in the butt for you.

The Zen master Seung Sahn would receive many long letters from his students. This was pre–e-mail, in the 1970s, so the letters would arrive by post and he would read them and often give very pointed but helpful information in response to their questions. One letter went on and on all about the various ways the student was overthinking his life and meditation practice. Seung Sahn took that letter and wrote his reply in big bold letters at the bottom of it, then mailed it back. Here is what he said:

WHAT ARE YOU?
TOMORROW YOU MAY DIE.
WHAT CAN YOU DO?
—S.S.[15]

Here is my spontaneous commentary:

What are you?
Who are you? What do you want to be? Who do you want to help?

Tomorrow you may die.
This is true and important to contemplate. Don't wallow in this idea or romanticize it. Just know you might get hit by a bus and people would be very, very sad. All the things you would like to do when you are not so hungover and indulgent and heart-broken, like write that life-changing book, or have a beautiful family, or whatever big dream it may be, can help many people and society overall. Don't give up on life. We're all waiting for you to come back to us and we're cheering you on, even if we don't say so all the time.

What can you do?
What can you do today? What are you going to do today? Go do it.

IF YOU ARE FEELING ANGRY

It's okay to feel angry. It really, truly is.

I've often struggled with anger, looking at it as a negative emotion that I need to be rid of. When I was nineteen years old I attended a two-month meditation retreat where we studied traditional Tibetan Buddhist texts. One of them was Gampopa's *Jewel Ornament of Liberation*. Lineage-wise, Gampopa is like my great (x37) grand-teacher, a holder of the Kagyu line of Tibetan Buddhism. The *Jewel Ornament of Liberation* serves as a foundational guide for everything from finding a teacher to attaining Buddhahood. In the text, Gampopa details the various realms that one may be reborn in, including the many types of hell realms.

Yes, even in Buddhism there's a belief that you can be reborn in a hell realm. There are hot hells where you get poked and burned. There are cold realms that are freezing and painful. There are all sorts of creative hells you can go to. And how do you get there? By one moment of anger. That's what it says! One moment of anger dooms you to a lifetime of hell. Then, after a very long lifetime, you get the chance to be reborn in another realm—ideally one that's not hell-like.

I don't know if I ascribe to the six-realms-of-rebirth thing (and that may mean I'm not a very traditional Buddhist, which I've made my peace with). I do know anger can be debilitating and can cause me to lash out at people. I know most of the anger I feel is internal; either stories I tell myself where I imagine expressing anger to someone or simply beating myself up. I've gotten a lot better at managing anger but I'm no saint.

Here's my middle-of-the-road advice, knowing that we all feel anger at some point but also knowing how paralyzing that emotion can be: Feel the anger. Let it wash over you like a wave. But don't feed it.

Anger is like fire. If you pour fuel on a fire it will continue to burn. Without fuel it will do its thing and then burn out. Anger is fueled by the stories we tell ourselves. The more revenge fantasies and elaborate plans you develop to show someone how awesome you are and how dumb they are, the longer that anger will burn. Without those stories anger burns for an appropriate amount of time and then dies out. Assuming you don't want to lie in bed late at night paralyzed by anger, here's how to do that:

Drop the story line.

That's it. When you notice that you are feeling anger, it's going to be accompanied by story lines about someone you feel angry at, ways you or other people were wronged, ideas on how to fix the situation, elaborate plans on how to get someone back, and more. Don't perpetuate those stories. Notice them. You can even acknowledge them by saying "It's okay to feel this" and then just feel the emotion boiling right beneath the surface. That's the juicy part.

Feel the emotion.

Stay with it.

When you notice you're drifting off into stories again, stop. Come back to feeling the emotion.

Feel your anger, and when it's done let it be done. You may get angry again, and that's okay, too.

IF YOU WANT TO KNOW HOW THE BUDDHA HANDLED ANGER

One day the Buddha was passing through a village and he sat down with his large monastic following to rest. He began to teach and as soon as the Buddha started talking many people gathered around to hear him.

One grumpy man was on the outskirts. Maybe he was mad about the Buddha blocking local traffic or was just sick of seeing spiritual teachers coming through his small town. He began to yell at the Buddha, accusing him of being a charlatan.

The Buddha wasn't fazed by this attack though. He remained ever-loving and calm. Finally, when the guy wouldn't shut up, he asked a simple question of the grumpy man. "If you purchased a gift for someone," the Buddha inquired, "but that person did not accept the gift, to whom would it belong?"

The man was taken by surprise by this question. "I guess it would still belong to me, because I bought it, right?"

"That's exactly right," said the Buddha. "In the same way, if you offer me anger but I don't accept your curses and accusations, not getting angry in return, then isn't the anger you offer returned to you, its owner?"

The grumpy man was overwhelmed and bowed to the Buddha. The Buddha continued, "As a mirror reflects an object, as a still lake reflects the sky—take care that what you speak or act is for good. For goodness will always cast back goodness, and harm will always cast back harm."[16]

That is the power of relinquishing anger, whenever possible.

IF YOU FEEL LIKE YOU ARE IN HELL

I hear you. I want to encourage you to aim to switch your view. The Zen teacher Suzuki Roshi once said, "Hell is not punishment, it's training."[17]

What are you training for? We don't know (yet). But you will down the road. That much I know.

IF YOU NEED TO HEAR A JOKE

A guy comes home to his roommate and immediately notices that his roommate now has a pumpkin for a head. He tries to gracefully broach the topic but the man comes right out and addresses it: "I found a lamp today, rubbed it, and a genie came out, offering me three wishes."

"Wow!" says his friend. "What did you wish for first?"

"The first wish, I asked for a million dollars."

"What happened?"

The pumpkin-headed fellow grabbed a few duffel bags and threw them at his friend, who unzipped them only to find stacks of hundred-dollar bills.

"Amazing! What did you wish for next?"

"The second wish, I wished for beautiful people to fool around with any time I want."

"What happened?"

The pumpkin-headed fellow threw open his bedroom door to reveal a number of beautiful people, splayed out naked and passed out on his bed.

"Wow! What happened with the third wish?"

"The third wish, I have to admit, I sorta messed up," said the man. "I wished for a pumpkin head."

IF YOU NEED TO HEAR A LESS BIZARRE JOKE

The Buddha walks into a bar and orders a martini, straight up. The bartender makes it and passes it to him. The Buddha hands the bartender a twenty-dollar bill and then waits. And waits. And waits. Finally the Buddha politely signals the bartender and asks, "Excuse me, can't I get my change?"

"Buddy," the bartender replies, "you of all people should know: change comes from within."[18]

IF YOU FEEL LIKE CONTACTING THAT PERSON

We live in a time when you can contact the person who has caused you heartbreak in a million different ways. You can find where they are through Instagram and go "accidentally" bump into them on the street. You can call, Skype, or Google Hangout them. You can passive-aggressively broadcast how awesome your life is without them across multiple social media platforms so as to make them jealous. Or you can just text them nonsense while drunk at 3 a.m.

Often when we reach out to the person who has caused us heartbreak it's not because we want to clear the air or finalize things so we can move on. We do it because we want something from them. We have lost the way we normally interact with that person so we're bargaining with them for some semblance of what we used to have. We might want that person back in our life, or at least long for them to feel some of the pain we feel or to see what they are missing out on by no longer being around us. We are essentially trying to get them to do something, anything, in relationship with us, because the previous ways of relating have fallen apart.

When you notice the itch to contact this individual, don't feel like you have to scratch it. Just pause. Look at the motivation for why you want to reach out to this person. Is it because you have something meaningful you want to say? Or are you trying to leverage your situation to lure this person into reconnecting with you in any way, positive or negative, just for some temporary sense of relief?

If your motivation isn't clear or very good, take a deep breath. Put down the iPhone. Place your hand on your heart and reconnect with your body. This might be a good time to meditate, exercise, or, at the very least, skim around this or another book that offers alternatives to acting out in habitual ways. The itch will go away if you can refrain from scratching it.

IF YOU FEEL REALLY, REALLY DEPRESSED

When Robin Williams killed himself I decided to come out of the closet as someone who has been, in the past, suicidal. I finally made up my mind to say something somewhere around the twentieth time I heard someone comment, "I never thought someone like him would do a thing like that."

When we say that we can't imagine "someone like him" we mean we can't imagine someone we have perceived to be joyful, successful, to—frankly—have their act together, to be so depressed that suicide would become a viable option to them. In other words, we think other people have their act together when, in fact, we're all suffering. Every single person you have ever met is fighting a battle right now. More often than not it's internal—them grappling with their own fear, insecurity, or depression. Sometimes it's more visible. But everyone has something they are suffering through so please be kind to them. Yet if you are suffering from depression and/or have suicidal thoughts you know that it's hard to care for yourself or others.

In 2012, after my life fell apart in a number of ways, I was indeed suicidal. There I was, the author of a best-selling Buddhist book, serving as a meditation teacher who was invited to speak at all sorts of fancy places. Yet I was struggling with the loss of my fiancée, my job, and most significantly one of my best friends. I was bowled over. I'd like to tell you I brought this triple whammy of a heartbreak to the meditation cushion but I couldn't do it; I was barely getting out of bed.

In order to function, I began to self-medicate in a destructive way. I knew better, but the vastness of my depression consumed any thoughts around self-care and regular meditation. I cannot explain how fathomless my sadness was during that period. I had a roof I would go up to every single day and contemplate jumping. I convinced myself that my first book was out there helping people, so maybe it would be a good idea, before I killed myself, to finish the second one my publisher had asked me to write. I sat down and wrote the second half of that book. It gave me purpose, and during that short period of time friends started to catch on that something was wrong with me and inquire about how to help.

I remember a day when I was particularly low. My friend Laura asked me to dinner but I could not stand to be in a restaurant, surrounded by people who were functioning normally. We sat on the grass in a nearby park as it got dark, with homeless people urinating nearby and the rats slowly coming out to play. She was very patient with me, as I was not interested in leaving. Finally she asked the question: "Have you ever thought about hurting yourself?" I broke down in tears and within the week was guided by her and others into therapy. A week later I returned to the meditation cushion. A week after that I began eating regularly. A week after that I finally got a full night's sleep. I'd like to think that the sections in this book on how to meditate, or "If You Feel Like You Can't Eat," or "If You Feel Like You Can't Sleep," will help you but if you are significantly depressed you may need more help than just this book. You may need therapy or medication or both.

Yes I am a big proponent of meditation as a tool for relating fully with your heartbreak. That said, meditation is not a cure-all for mental illness. The Buddha never taught a discourse titled "Don't Help Yourself, Continue to Suffer Your Chemical Imbalance." If you have a mental illness, meditation may be helpful, but it should be considered an addition to, not a substitution for, prescribed medication.

While I do not suffer from clinical depression, I will say that my life turned around because I sought help. Buddhists can't just take everything to the meditation cushion and hope it will work out. When things get tough, as in reaching the point of can't-imagine-getting-out-of-bed-in-the-morning tough, you need help. And there should be no shame in seeking it. If you even remotely feel like you are struggling with depression, or are going through an emotional time that simply feels out of control, the best way to take care of yourself is to seek guidance from trained professionals. Sure that can be a meditation teacher, but a therapist may prove more helpful at that point. Therapy in and of itself can be treated as a mindfulness practice, where you bring your full attention for an hour at a time to what is expressing itself in your body and your mind.

In all things heartbreak, please don't feel like you have to go it alone. Meditation does not preclude or diminish the power of therapeutic methods. They are powerful in their own right. There are trained people out there who can work with you to navigate your suffering. Do not be scared to seek help.

When you do, you may find that this moment, this totally devastating moment of true darkness, is one where you will be changed. You may end up with some scars on your heart, but some good may ultimately come out of it, too. As Pema Chödrön once said, "In reality when you feel depressed, lonely, betrayed, or any unwanted feelings, this is an important moment on the spiritual path. This is where real transformation can take place."[19] I can't promise you will wake up one day and feel the same as you did before whatever happened occurred, but I can promise that real transformation is happening to you, right now.

Just because Robin Williams was a comedian, a celebrity, or someone we viewed as a joyful person did not mean he wasn't fighting demons unknown to us. I share my story in the same vein; the fact that I struggled with suicidal thoughts does not negate my years of meditation experience or understanding of the Buddhist teachings, but it shows that I am human and fall prey to suffering like all humans do. You can be well-practiced and still struggle like anyone else. Robin Williams ended up taking his life. I was lucky in that I was able to seek help and no longer feel the way I once did. In fact, that experience only deepened my appreciation for the practice of meditation and the Buddhist teachings. In many ways, my life has been transformed. Yours will be, too.

IF YOU FEEL THAT IT'S TIME TO FORGIVE

There are two types of forgiveness that often accompany heartbreak. The first is the desire to forgive someone who has wronged you in some way. The other is the yearning to forgive yourself, which is actually the foundation of forgiveness overall in my experience.

I am, by nature, not an angry person. I'm not quick to build a case against someone else and then write them out of my life. I am not a yeller. I feel uncomfortable bad-mouthing people. But when someone does something really cruel to a loved one, or something that I think will hurt a lot of people, I get fiercely protective, and I get pretty upset at that person.

When I get upset, I find that time and space soothe me. I am able to forgive, not right away, but in a matter of weeks or months. This is, incidentally, likely linked to my daily meditation practice, which includes a regular act of forgiveness.

When you're meditating, you have a constant chance for forgiveness. You sit there with the desire to remain focused on the breath. But what happens? You drift off into thought instead. In that moment you can berate yourself, thinking you're the worst meditator of all time, or you can simply forgive yourself for doing what you are habituated to doing: thinking. It's natural for the mind to think.

Just because thinking happens during meditation doesn't mean you are bad or wrong. It means you need to forgive yourself this totally minor transgression and come back to the breath. When we do this simple act of forgiving ourselves, we establish a stronger foundation for forgiving others.

Tibet's greatest saint is a gentleman who was known as Milarepa, who has a very powerful story around forgiveness. Milarepa had a sordid past. His father died when he was young, and his uncle and aunt took his entire family's fortune. He was so mad he ran off and studied black magic as a way to plot his revenge. He waited until his aunt and uncle were having a wedding party for their son and summoned a giant hailstorm, killing dozens of their guests. When the local villagers plotted to enact revenge on him, he found out and sent yet another hailstorm to their land, killing their crops and scaring them off.

As time went on, Milarepa began to realize that summoning hailstorms was not the most productive way to deal with his problems. He came to his senses, saw what harm he had caused, and felt tremendous remorse. He knew he needed help in order to atone for what he had done. He had heard of a Buddhist teacher named Marpa and set out to find him. When he did, though, he discovered that Marpa was not going to just give him a free pass after he killed all those people. Marpa said he had to pay for the teachings he would receive, and the form of that payment would be intense physical labor.

Under Marpa's guidance, Milarepa built a huge tower made out of stone, all by himself. Months later, when it was done, Marpa wandered over, pointed at a gap, and said, "Why did you put windows in there? I didn't ask for windows." Even though he did; Marpa definitely had asked for windows. But Milarepa wouldn't argue. He took the tower down, brick by brick, and rebuilt it according to Marpa's instructions for the next several months. Then Marpa would come by and tell him he did it all wrong again and down the tower would come. This was repeated multiple times; with Milarepa putting in years of grueling labor—hard time, so to speak—to atone for his misdeeds.

Marpa eventually revealed that this whole affair had been a way to give Milarepa the time and space he needed in order to forgive himself. At that point Marpa was able to offer him spiritual teachings, but not before. If Milarepa had been offered teachings before, he would have been seeing them through the lens of what a wretched murdering son-of-a-bitch he was. After all the work Milarepa engaged in, working to forgive himself, he was able to cherish and follow the teachings wholeheartedly, and he quickly attained enlightenment and made amends with those he had previously hurt. But the first step was forgiving himself.

If Milarepa was able to eventually work through his guilt and self-loathing, we can, too. We may find the same thing he did, in fact, which is our innate wisdom and tender but strong heart. Milarepa is often depicted with a small smile playing across his face. Having learned to forgive, he experienced true joy and enlightenment. We can, too.

Even if you're not interested in spiritual enlightenment, you at least want to be able to forgive your ex or that friend who wronged you. The more we lay the ground for forgiveness with ourselves, the more we are able to offer forgiveness to others.

IF YOU FEEL RELIEF-GUILT

I have a meditation student; we'll call him Ronny. Ronny and I talk about how his meditation practice is going but also how he's seeing it show up in various parts of his life—including his romantic life. A while ago I saw him start to move toward a breakup. When it finally happened he admitted something to me that I've heard a million times before. He felt a small sense of relief having finally ended his relationship, right up alongside the sadness, frustration, and many other emotions. But because he felt that relief, he felt guilt, too.

I've seen this so often I think it deserves its own category of heartbreak emotions: relief-guilt. Relief-guilt is when we part from something or someone and feel a bit liberated but, because either we feel we should be suffering or the other person is currently suffering, we feel guilty.

You feel how you feel. That's neither good nor bad. The only bad emotion, in my opinion, is the one you close yourself off to. If you feel relief, feel relief. If guilt arises, notice that, but don't let it prevent you from feeling relief. And remember that no one needs to know how you feel but you. Unless you put up a billboard I can't imagine anyone will see relief floating off you. You can feel that without pissing anyone off. Again, it's good to feel what you feel.

Another thing to remember is that just because you have conflicting emotions it doesn't mean you're a bad person. Here's something I've never publicly admitted but will now write into a book: I felt relief-guilt when my father died. He had been sick for half my lifetime and, by the time he passed, his mind was starting to go. I know for a fact that this was his worst nightmare; he used his body to get around but prided himself on his clever and insightful mind. When he lost the ability to express himself clearly I began to suspect it was a painful experience for him. When he died not too long after, I wailed and yelled in grief. But after that, there was a sliver of relief. I felt so guilty for feeling that, but it's how I felt and I'll be damned if it makes me a worse son.

There are some things we should feel guilty about. If you cheated on your partner or cut a person out of your heart, I'm not going to tell you not to feel guilty. But at some point you will need to forgive yourself. Instead of relief-guilt you will feel guilt-guilt but ultimately find relief from it. If you need to forgive, I recommend flipping to the section titled "If You Feel That It's Time to Forgive."

Our emotions have a lot to teach us. Relief might be teaching us that we made the right decision. Embracing this emotional state helps us move closer toward healing. Like Ronny you may find it's okay to feel conflicting emotions and that, like all things, they change and morph over time into something brand new.

IF YOU FEEL LIKE YOU'LL NEVER TRUST AGAIN

Coming from a Buddhist background I think trust is an interesting thing. Within Buddhism we don't have external deities we put our trust in, thinking those beings will save us; it's a nontheistic religious tradition. Even the most complex of visualizations within the Tibetan Buddhist system are representative of qualities we have within us. Thus, when we practice various forms of meditation what we are developing trust in is our own innate wisdom.

As I mentioned earlier, when it comes to love, we have to layer our foundation of trust in ourselves before we can really offer trust to other beings. If you've been in a long relationship and that person disappeared into the night, seemingly with no explanation, you may wonder if what you felt all these months or years was real. You might begin to no longer trust in your own experience, thinking that maybe you've been delusional all this time, making up all the joy and love that relationship held.

You're not delusional. Whatever you feel is what you feel, and that is normal. That is your subjective reality. Just because someone left you does not mean that your subjective reality is invalid. It just means that what was going on for them shifted in ways unexpected to you, and while that's a bummer it's no reason to no longer have faith in yourself and your experience.

As time heals your particular set of wounds you will find yourself developing trust in yourself again. You may pick up a photo of the two of you and remember sweet things that person told you that day. Or you may sit down and recall some of the really amazing aspects about yourself, like your sense of humor or the fact that you're actually a pretty kind person. Or you may be at a bar and your friend will nudge you and say, "Why didn't you give him your phone number? He was flirting with you." In these moments you'll realize what's apparent to the rest of us: that you're still a valuable, wonderful, vibrant being who people find desirable. And maybe, just maybe, you'll actually believe me when I say that you shouldn't give up trust in yourself. You can begin to reestablish a foundation of trust in your innate goodness, based in becoming familiar with all of who you are.

Then there's the flip side of the trust equation—because you've been hurt by someone you're not sure if you can trust other people. Sure that guy was flirting with you, but he's probably as big of a jerk as your ex, if not bigger. Why should you let yourself be even minutely vulnerable around him?

Listen, I understand where you might have trust issues. I do. But at some point you're going to have to let people into your heart because, well, it's the way of things. As you heal you will find a certain amount of joy that comes from connecting with other people and with that connection comes trust. Wanting to offer our heart to others is natural to the human experience. We all love love. We all long to connect openly and authentically. So you will find yourself in the position of potentially trusting others, and my guess is that you will give them a chance.

You can kick and fight and scream against trusting again—whether that means trusting yourself or others—but people will continue to try to connect with you and at some point your heart will naturally open to them. This doesn't negate the fact that you have been hurt before, but it also doesn't mean you're destined to repeat the same mistakes that came before.

I once heard that in response to a question about the Buddhist concept of karma the Tibetan Buddhist master Chögyam Trungpa Rinpoche simply responded, "Everything is predetermined . . . until now." The fact that you might have trouble trusting is predetermined by all the pain you have experienced in the past. But now, in this very moment, you can choose to open your heart and trust again.

IF YOU FEEL LIKE YOU HAVE NO RIGHT TO BE HEARTBROKEN

You do. We can't change the way we feel. Sometimes that means loving someone we wish we didn't love. Sometimes that means being heartbroken about something that is simply baffling to us. My dear friend Ellie climbed into my storefront window/office while I was writing this book. She asked if I was going to talk about how some of the greatest heartbreaks come from some of the shortest incidents. I think that's a good point; thanks, Ellie.

In my life there have been two types of romantic relationships. One type burns hot and quick, and ends right as I'm starting to get to know that person. The other begins that way but eases into a comfortable companionship accompanied by mind-blowing and fun sex. That said, I have found that the length of time a relationship lasts is irrelevant in terms of the amount of heartbreak you end up with.

There's some stupid rule of thumb I heard long ago where the amount of time you're supposed to need in terms of healing your broken heart is proportionate to the length of time you were with that person. The magic equation is that it will take half the amount of time you were in a relationship for you to fully heal from that relationship. So if you were with someone for a year it should supposedly take you six months to get over that person.

I think that equation is malarky. I have gotten out of long relationships where it felt like it was a natural ending point with that person and, after we spent the appropriate amount of time mourning together, I was able to move on relatively easily. There was simply more space created for us to process and accept the breakup. In contrast I was once in a four-month relationship that ended abruptly and I was devastated. Part of the devastation was my own misunderstanding of where that relationship was going, including my set ideas of what the future would hold for us as a couple. Part of it was me being frustrated and feeling that this person didn't give the relationship a real chance. There was a lot swirling around in my mind but the point is that the relationship was over before it began and the episode knocked me on my back. So the whole "the amount of heartbreak time is half the time of the relationship" thing is baloney, in my experience.

Also, you have every right to feel heartbroken about things that, conventionally, may not appear to be a big deal. I can't tell you the number of people who came to see me with the intent of telling a romantic story but ended up telling me about the death of a family member or animal companion. Because it was a long time ago or "just a cat" they felt like maybe they had no right to feel so much pain but it was there and I was honored to witness it.

No matter what you feel heartbroken about, and no matter how long ago something happened, it's okay to feel the way that you feel.

IF YOU WONDER WHAT HAPPENS WHEN A LOVED ONE DIES

I will be the first to admit I know nothing about what happens after death. I know death well. A significant percentage of the beings I've loved have died. I am writing this particular section of the book the day after my beloved dog died. I am sitting here, processing, and the one question that comes up, one that I cannot answer, is, what happens to her now?

I don't know. I should toe the Buddhist party line and say that she will be reborn in one of six realms of existence: the god realm, the jealous god realm, the human realm, or she might become an animal again, suffer as a hungry ghost, or end up in the hell realms. If these realms exist, I hope she can be reborn as a human and practice the dharma. That is said to be the best place to be reborn, because humans can use their minds to work toward enlightenment, thus freeing themselves from the continuous cycle of suffering. But I don't know for sure whether these realms exist because I have only seen the human and animal ones for myself. Here is what I do know:

· she lived a good life
· we spent a lot of quality time together
· she knew she was loved

Somehow, even in the midst of this incredible grief and pain, that's comforting to me. If you have recently lost a loved one, I encourage you to consider whether you can say those three things. If so, that is a good death, in my mind.

IF YOU FEEL IT'S TIME TO LET THEM GO

One of the wisest beings I know, Sakyong Mipham Rinpoche, once gave a pithy equation for how to let go of the painful aspects of our experience: "Love mixed with space is called letting go."[20]

If you yearn to let go of your pain, increase one or both of these things and see what happens.

IF SOCIETY HAS BROKEN YOUR HEART

First things first: society has broken my heart, too. I don't know when you'll be reading this book. Right now I am heartbroken by the rampant police brutality that has resulted in the deaths of way too many people of color. I am heartbroken by the giant gap between the rich and the poor. I am heartbroken that our political system is, in my opinion, pretty damn broken. Maybe you are reading this at a time when the daily news is about how our alien overlords have really skewed the border situation so Earthers can't get decent jobs. I don't know. But if you are feeling heartbroken about the major societal issues in the world and I happen to still be alive please know that at this moment I too am heartbroken, so you are not alone.

With so much suffering in the world, it can be easy to lean into your heartbreak only to get completely overwhelmed. I feel that way sometimes.

When I feel overwhelmed I remember something my root teacher, Sakyong Mipham Rinpoche, once said about society. He said that society can be two people having tea. I've thought a lot about that. If you and I sat down to have tea we have at least two choices for how we spend our time together. We could either bash others, slandering them entirely, and complain about our various aches and pains and who's to blame for them. Or we could sit down and share our hearts, talking about what we are doing to help others or better our neighborhoods. In the former we might be more prone to whipping out our phones and ignoring each other, generating habitual patterns that are based in fear and distraction. With the latter we might find ourselves being fully present and authentic with one another. In either case, we are creating society over tea.

Then a funny thing happens. We go out into the world and take part in other societies. Maybe you go home to your family, which is a society made up of you, your partner, maybe some kids. And I go into my meditation studio and work with employees and students, which is its own little society.

When we do that we bring the energy from our tea with us. If we have been distracted jerks over tea, perpetuating negative emotional states, you might walk in and snap at your spouse. Meanwhile I might be oblivious and self-involved in dealing with meditation students. If instead we were authentic over tea you might walk in the door and say, "Hey honey, how are you?" and ask it in a way that softens her heart and solicits an honest answer. I might walk into work and lead a meditation class that connects with where the participants are and what they might need to hear.

Then your partner and my meditation students take that energy and go out into the world in one way or another, based on our interaction. Thus our tea society affected your family and my work societies, and the ways we showed up for those societies affected the way those individuals we encountered went on to the other societies they are part of.

Robert Kennedy once gave a beautiful speech where he made the point that our actions are like a stone thrown in a pool of water; we don't know where the ripples are going to go. We may never be able to see the complete ramifications of all of our actions in society.[21] But we do know how our mini societies feel when we bring our full, authentic self to them. They feel a lot better than if we were to bring our jerk-self to them. Here are a few types of societies you may not have thought of as actual, fully fledged societies:

· your family
· the place you volunteer
· your romantic relationship
· your workplace
· that club you participate in
· your yoga, workout, or meditation community

Think about those societies. How do you normally show up for them? How do you cocreate them?

What do I mean by cocreate? Good question. Take Nicole for example. She's a longtime meditation student of mine who is a nurse practitioner with a loving family. One day over Google Hangouts she was lamenting that she couldn't spend more time with her family at night because people at work e-mailed her until all hours of the night. She expressed a desire for that to stop.

I perked up a bit. "How many people work in your office?" I asked.

"Ten," she said.

So let's do the math. Nicole is one-tenth of her work society. That work society has a shared value already in place: we are productive and one of the ways we show that is by always being reachable by e-mail. Nicole thinks that's not a good shared value; she would like to be productive but not at the expense of downtime. If she turned to a coworker and they agreed that they shouldn't e-mail about work into all hours of the night then something new would emerge: 20 percent of that society would be against the constant e-mailing policy. If someone else overheard them talking about this in the break room and jumped on board in agreement, 30 percent of that society would have rebelled against this one ingrained work policy. That 30 percent can bring it up at a meeting and maybe that percentage jumps up to a majority and people stop e-mailing after 5 P.M.

I mention this one example because Nicole initially approached this as something out of her control—believing that she couldn't opt out of e-mailing people back at 8 P.M. Yet here's the simple truth: we are always creating society. Every time we interact with someone we are creating society. Also, the way we show up in our smaller societies has an impact on society overall.

E-mailing after work hours may seem minor but that's ten people who are now free to do whatever they find meaningful in their evenings. Maybe one of those people is more able to help out at church or at an animal shelter. Maybe they do some profound work outside of their nine-to-five, and they're now freed up to create the next great invention. I don't know where the ripples of that particular stone may go, but I bet it will be a positive thing. Something as simple as changing an e-mail policy at work may prove to be very vast in its ripple effect.

When you feel overwhelmed by how to change some of the major systemic issues of our time, I implore you to keep your heart open and show up as authentically as you can for others. It makes a bigger difference than you know. When you do that you affect society, in small and ultimately in big ways.

Incidentally, I was invited to speak to staff at the White House this year. It was like most offices I visit; the staff were delightful but totally stressed out. I gave the basic meditation instruction offered in this book in the hopes of their hearts softening. But then I told them what I just wrote here and the knowledge that they cocreate their (very powerful) office environment was what allowed them to relax. I'm not saying this to brag or pat myself on the back. I'm saying this to make it clear that the more we realize how we participate in creating society and the more positive stones we throw, the bigger those ripples might become.

IF YOU CAN STILL OFFER LOVE

There are many stories of people going through heartbreak and somehow, miraculously, not closing their heart off to the people whom they are breaking up with or have been wronged by. It's impressive, I know. While I was at ABC Carpet & Home a fifty-seven-year-old man named David came to meet with me and shared one of those stories.

David met Donna while they were still in high school. They fell in love and lost their virginity to one another. It was magical that they had met so young; it meant that they had their whole lives to be together. They made plans to attend the same college. Donna was a year ahead of David in school so she left town but they remained a couple, intending to make the whole long-distance thing work. David couldn't make the long trek out to visit her at college until a few months into her freshman year, but when he did, he enjoyed the five-hour bus ride, eager to see her and reconnect.

Yet when David arrived, something was off. The mood was all wrong. He was putting out love vibes but did not sense that love was being echoed back to him. Her roommate had cleared out for the night to give them space, so he was excited to think they might hop into bed together. Maybe things were turning around. But when they returned to her room that night she broke up with him.

While David was still on the plan they had set up together, Donna had created a whole new life at college, one that included a new boyfriend two years her senior. "His name is Ray," she said. The way David said those words to me in 2015, I could tell it was the same intonation Donna had used forty years earlier, an intonation that was etched in his mind after playing it on repeat, day after day, for longer than David might care to admit. Donna went to Ray's room that night, leaving David to sob in her bed. His whole life plan had been ruined, and he had lost what he believed to be the love of his life. "I thought the world was ending," he said. The next morning, Donna sent Ray to check on David. David awoke to find Ray's dog licking his face, with Ray laughing nearby.

David went home and suffered from immense heartbreak. One of the worst parts was knowing that, because he had applied through early admission and had been accepted, he would end up at the same school with Donna and Ray the next year. He decided to not give up entirely on Donna. When he next saw her he offered her friendship and humor. The romantic part of the relationship was dead and being mourned, but David wasn't going to let go of the notion of having any relationship at all.

Donna and David's friendship endured. Donna and Ray broke up eventually. She married someone else, as did David. They remained so close that they were in each other's wedding parties. When their children were born they became godparents to the other person's kids. When David told her he was going to come share his story with me she asked, "Can it still be heartbreak if so much good came out of it?"

In my opinion, it can. Heartbreak is real, even if it's not always a permanent scar. David is quite rare in being willing and able to rebound from such a loss and still offer his love to the woman who hurt him. But I'm glad he did. Because it's an excellent testimonial to how love can morph and be life-changing in new ways. As David told me, all of his great loves sprang out of that initial experience. It was heartbreak and a lot of good came out of it. And he still calls Donna every December 8th, on the anniversary of the night they lost their virginity.

IF YOU FEEL ACCEPTANCE

At some point even your heartbreak will change and you will begin to make peace with what has occurred. I remember speaking with a mother whose son had died at a young age. She was devastated for a very long time, she told me, but a few years after his death she found herself occasionally smiling while in the company of good friends and family. She felt guilty that she was starting to accept the terrible loss of her son. Yet she also copped to the fact that she knew her son would want her to be happy and to smile as much as possible. She was moving toward acceptance of this tragedy.

Whatever acceptance looks like for you, it's perfectly fine. There may be many small waves of acceptance that add up to your heart slowly healing or it might be a big lightbulb going off over your head in a realization that means you've finally come to terms with what has happened. In either case, I am glad your heart is on the mend.

A REMINDER TO CHERISH YOUR LIFE

Like all things, this life is temporary. If you're reading this you were lucky enough to wake up to another day. You can do any number of things with
this day. You can wallow in heartbreak. You can
treat yourself with a modicum of kindness. You can
connect wholeheartedly with others. There are
many things you can do. Please cherish your life.

A TRAINING FOR FUTURE
HEARTBREAK

Late one night while I was writing this book, my friend Brett called me on his way to the airport. He works for the U.S. State Department and, as a result, is often assigned to diplomatic posts around the world for a few years at a time. I have known Brett for over a decade and we are quite close. I had just gotten attached to the idea of having him back state-side, where I can see him every month or so.

"I am on my way to the flight," he said. I realized what day it was and that this was the "good-bye, I am flying to go live in Dubai for three years" call. We chatted for twenty minutes, ending with straightfor-ward and manly "I'll miss you's" and "I love you's." When I hung up the phone I felt a twinge of heart-break over not being able to see one of my best friends for a long, long time.

And I sat with it. I let it exist. I didn't fight it. And I'm okay.

I was slated to go out to dinner with my partner, and I told her what had happened. I talked it through honestly and gave voice to the heartbreak, without perpetuating a lot of the story line around it. I didn't say, "He'll make lots of new friends and never care if he sees me again" or "Our friendship is doomed" or any of those weird doubt-filled thoughts that flitted across my mind.

I stayed with my heartbreak all night, giving it the space it needed. I ate well. I slept longer than I usually do. I took a long walk the next morning. And I can say that by taking care of myself this little heartbreak has passed through my system. I will miss my friend, but also I will be okay. The love I feel remains.

We can train for the big heartbreaks in our life by being with all of the little heartbreaks that come up. By giving these little heartbreaks the attention they need instead of squashing them down or running from them, we see our way through them. That builds confidence that we can, indeed, see our way through to healing heartbreak in general.

The next time someone close to me dies (as I know they will) or a breakup occurs (as I fear it might) or I get knocked on my ass by some other form of heartbreak (as is the nature of life) I will have trained to open my heart and give myself the space and care needed to accommodate this loss. But that will happen only if I stick to the training of really caring for each smaller heartbreak that comes my way.

Our whole life is a training in heartbreak, whether we acknowledge it or not. By showing up for it, day in and day out, we learn to make it a part of our spiritual path as opposed to something we have to hide from. Thus, we show up for our life more authentically and offer our love that much more deeply. Heartbreak becomes not a horrific thing we have to run from, but the very path to transforming our life into one marked by love.

A Dedication of Merit

May all beings who encounter this book be free
   from suffering
May these words aid those in need
May those who are touched by this book open
   their hearts fully to others
May we all create a benevolent society based in
   mindfulness and compassion

NOTES

1. Sakyong Mipham Rinpoche, *Ruling Your World: Ancient Strategies for Modern Life* (New York: Harmony, 2006), 139.
2. Thich Nhat Hanh, *Fidelity: How to Create a Loving Relationship that Lasts* (Berkeley, CA: Parallax Press, 2011), 81.
3. Pema Chödrön, *The Places That Scare You* (Boston: Shambhala Publications, 2001), 47.
4. If you would like to be guided in this practice by Lodro you can visit his YouTube channel and watch a video of this instruction: www.youtube.com/lodrorinzler
5. Confession: this is a true story. Brussels sprouts are delicious. I can't believe I went without them for so many years.
6. His Holiness the Karmapa, Ogyen Trinley Dorje, *The Heart Is Noble: Changing the World from the Inside Out* (Boston: Shambhala Publications, 2013), 27.
7. David Chadwick, ed., *Zen Is Right Here: Teaching Stories and Anecdotes of Shunryu Suzuki* (Boston: Shambhala Publications, 2007), 37.
8. Pema Chödrön, *Living Beautifully* (Boston: Shambhala Publications, 2012), 3.

9. Seung Sahn, *Only Don't Know* (Boston: Shambhala Publications, 1982), 83.
10. Thich Nhat Hanh, 55.
11. The nonprofit leadership training I founded, the Institute for Compassionate Leadership, was established as a direct result of my desire to create more compassionate leaders like Alex. The meditation studio I co-founded, MNDFL, only came to being because Ellie Burrows, a volunteer at the institute, talked me into starting it with her.
12. Is this the first Buddhist book that talks about swinging while on ecstasy? It might be.
13. David Chadwick, ed., 11.
14. His Holiness the Karmapa, 32.
15. Seung Sahn, 20.
16. Traditional tale adapted from Sarah Conover, *Kindness: A Treasury of Buddhist Wisdom for Children and Parents* (Boston: Skinner House, 2001), 47–48.
17. David Chadwick, ed., 28.
18. I have now, five books later, concluded the joke I started with my first book's title, *The Buddha Walks into a Bar.* I don't know about you, but I feel relieved to have that done with.
19. Pema Chödrön, *Practicing Peace* (Boston: Shambhala Publications, 2007), 57–58.
20. Sakyong Mipham Rinpoche, 143
21. It's been said that you can see all of your karma, including the totality of how your actions have had ramifications, if you become a fully enlightened Buddha. If you do that please let me know how it goes because I am very curious.

RESOURCES

Movies

Sometimes you can't just sit there with your hand on your heart feeling all your many feelings. You might yearn for some distraction. Here are some movies that I'd recommend over, say, drinking an entire bottle of whiskey and going on Tinder. (My favorite is *500 Days of Summer*.)

500 Days of Summer. Directed by Marc Webb. Fox Searchlight, 2009.

Brokeback Mountain. Directed by Ang Lea. Focus Features, 2005.

Casablanca. Directed by Michael Curtiz. Warner Brothers, 1942.

Crazy Stupid Love. Directed by Glenn Ficarra and John Requa. Carousel Productions II, 2011.

Eternal Sunshine of the Spotless Mind. Directed by Michel Gondry. Focus Features, 2004.

Forgetting Sarah Marshall. Directed by Nicholas Stoller. Universal Pictures, 2008.

Her. Directed by Spike Jonze. Annapurna Pictures, 2013.

High Fidelity. Directed by Stephen Frears. Touchstone Pictures, 2000.

It's a Wonderful Life. Directed by Frank Capra. Liberty Films II, 1947.

King Kong. Directed by John Guillermin. Dino De Laurentiis Company, 1976.

Kramer vs. Kramer. Directed by Robert Benton. Columbia Pictures, 1979.

Up. Directed by Peter Docter and Bob Peterson. Walt Disney Pictures, 2009.

Books about Meditation

Sit Like a Buddha, by Lodro Rinzler. Boston: Shambhala Publications, 2014.

Start Here Now: An Open-Hearted Guide to the Path and Practice of Meditation, by Susan Piver. Boston: Shambhala Publications, 2015.

Turning the Mind into an Ally, by Sakyong Mipham Rinpoche. New York: Riverhead, 2003.

Books about Buddhism

The Buddha Walks into a Bar: A Guide to Life for a New Generation, by Lodro Rinzler. Boston: Shambhala Publications, 2012.

The Heart Is Noble: Changing the World from the Inside Out, by His Holiness the Karmapa, Ogyen Trinley Dorje. Boston: Shambhala Publications, 2013.

The Heart of the Buddha: Entering the Tibetan Buddhist Path, by Chögyam Trungpa Rinpoche. Boston: Shambhala Publications, 1991.

Zen Mind, Beginner's Mind, by Shunryu Suzuki Roshi. New York: Weatherhill, 1970.

BOOKS ABOUT HEARTBREAK

How to Love Yourself (and Sometimes Other People): Spiritual Advice for Modern Relationships, by Lodro Rinzler and Meggan Watterson. Carlsbad, CA: Hay House, 2015.

This Is Where I Leave You, by Jonathan Tropper. New York: Dutton, 2009.

The Wisdom of a Broken Heart: Stop the Pain and Learn to Love Again, by Susan Piver. New York: Free Press, 2009.